CONTENTS

TABLE OF CASES v

PREFACE xiii

Chapter 1 THE NATURE OF TORTIOUS LIABILITY

| 1.1 | General principles of liability | 1 |
| 1.2 | Human rights and tort | 1 |

Chapter 2 NEGLIGENCE

2.1	Duty of care	4
2.2	Breach of the duty of care	8
2.3	Causation and remoteness of damage	17
2.4	Nervous shock	30
2.5	Pure economic loss	39
2.6	Negligent misstatement	40
2.7	Omissions	44

Chapter 3 OCCUPIERS' LIABILITY

| 3.1 | Liability to lawful visitors under the 1957 Act | 48 |
| 3.2 | Liability to trespassers under the 1984 Act | 54 |

Chapter 4 NUISANCE

| 4.1 | Private nuisance | 59 |
| 4.2 | Public nuisance | 69 |

Chapter 5 STRICT LIABILITY

| 5.1 | *Rylands v Fletcher* | 71 |
| 5.2 | Liability for animals | 80 |

Chapter 6 TRESPASS TO LAND

6.1   Potential claimants   86
6.2   Actions amounting to a trespass   86
6.3   The definition of 'land' in trespass   87
6.4   Trespass *ab initio*   89
6.5   Defences   90

Chapter 7 TORTS CONCERNING GOODS

7.1   Trespass to goods   91
7.2   Product liability   93

Chapter 8 TRESPASS TO THE PERSON

8.1   Assault   96
8.2   Battery   98
8.3   False imprisonment   104
8.4   Intentional indirect harm   107

Chapter 9 TORTS AFFECTING REPUTATION

9.1   Defamation   110
9.2   Malicious falsehood and deceit   118

Chapter 10 EMPLOYMENT-RELATED TORTS

10.1   Vicarious liability   122
10.2   Employers' liability   129
10.3   Breach of a statutory duty   134

Chapter 11 THE GENERAL DEFENCES

11.1   *Volenti non fit injuria*   136
11.2   Inevitable accident   137
11.3   Act of God   137
11.4   Illegality (*ex turpi causa non oritur actio*)   138
11.5   Contributory negligence   139

Index   140

TABLE OF CASES

Abouzaid v Mothercare (UK) Ltd [2001] EWCA Civ 348 ....91, 93
Addie v Dumbreck, *see* Robert Addie & Sons (Collieries) Ltd
  v Dumbreck
Alcock v Chief Constable of South Yorkshire
  [1992] 4 All ER 907 ....3, 33, 36
Allen v Gulf Oil Refining Ltd [1980] QB 156 ....58, 67
Anns v Merton London Borough Council
  [1978] AC 728 ....5, 40
Attorney-General v PYA Quarries Ltd
  [1957] 2 QB 169 ....58, 69

Baker v TE Hopkins [1959] 3 All ER 225 ....121, 132
Baker v Willoughby [1970] AC 467 ....20, 21
Barber v Somerset County Council
  [2004] UKHL 13 132
Barnett v Chelsea & Kensington Hospital
  Management Committee [1969] 1 QB 428 ....3, 17
Basely v Clarkson (1681) 3 Lev 37 ....85, 87
Bernstein v Skyviews *see* Lord Bernstein of
  Leigh v Skyviews & General Ltd
Bird v Jones (1845) 7 QB 742 ....95, 104
Blyth v Proprietors of the Birmingham
  Waterworks (1856) 11 Exch 781 ....3, 8
Bolam v Friern Hospital Management
  Committee [1957] 2 All ER 118 ....3, 14–17
Bolitho v City and Hackney Health Authority
  [1998] AC 232 16
Bolton v Stone [1951] AC 850 ....3, 10, 63
Bookbinder v Tebbitt [1989] 1 All ER 1169.....................109, 115
Bottomley v Todmorden Cricket Club [2003]
  EWCA Civ 1575...53
Bourhill v Young [1943] AC 92...32
Bradford Corporation v Pickles [1895] AC 587................................1
British Celanese v AH Hunt (Capacitors) Ltd
  [1969] 1 WLR 959 75
British Railways Board v Herrington [1972]
  AC 877 ....47, 54
Bux v Slough Metals [1974] 1 All ER 262.................................129
Byrne v Deane [1937] 1 KB 818 ....109, 112

C (Adult: Refusal of Medical Treatment),
    Re [1994] 1 WLR 290 103
Calascione v Dixon (1994) 19 BMLR 97 38
Cambridge Water Co v Eastern Counties
    Leather plc [1994] 2 WLR 53 ....70, 76, 78
Candler v Crane Christmas & Co [1951]
    2 KB 164...40, 41
Caparo Industries plc v Dickman [1990]
    2 AC 605; [1990] 1 All ER 568 ....3, 6, 43, 44
Carslogie Steamship Co v Royal Norwegian
    Government [1952] AC 292 24
Cassidy v Daily Mirror Newspapers Ltd [1929]
    2 KB 331...113
Castle v St Augustine Links (1922) 38 TLR 615 ....58, 69
Century Insurance Co Ltd v Northern Ireland
    Transport Board [1942] AC 509 125
Chaudhry v Prabhaker [1998] 3 All ER 718 41
Chester v Ashfar [2004] UKHL 41; [2005]
    1 AC 134...22
Christie v Davey [1893] 1 Ch 316..58, 61
Cole v Turner (1704) Holt KB 108 99
Collins v Wilcock [1984] 3 All ER 374........................95, 99, 100
Condon v Basi [1985] 2 All ER 453 101
Crown River Cruisers Ltd v Kimbolton
    Fireworks Ltd [1996] 2 Lloyd's Rep 533 ....58, 62
Cullen v Chief Constable of the Royal Ulster
    Constabulary [2003] 1 WLR 1763 135
Cummings v Grainger [1977] 1 All ER 104 ....81, 83
Curran v Northern Ireland Co-ownership Housing
    Association Ltd 1987 AC 718 5
Curtis v Betts [1990] 1 All ER 769 ....70, 82

Delaney v TP Smith & Co [1946] KB 393 ....85, 86
Derry v Peek (1889) 14 App Cas 337 ....109, 118
Dhesi v Chief Constable of the West Midlands
    Police (2000) *The Times,* 9 May 70, 84
Donoghue v Stevenson [1932] AC 562 ....4, 93
Doughty v Turner Manufacturing Co Ltd
    [1964] 1 QB 518...28
Draper v Hodder [1972] 2 QB 556..80
Dulieu v White & Sons [1901] 2 KB 669 31

Elias v Passmore [1934] 2 KB 164 89

F (Mental Patient: Sterilisation), *In re* [1990]
    2 AC 1..95, 102
Fairchild v Glenhaven Funeral Services Ltd and
    others; Fox v Spousal (Midlands) Ltd;
    Matthews v Associated Portland Cement Manufacturers

(1978) Ltd and another [2002] UKHL 22;
[2002] 3 WLR 89 ....3, 19
Fouldes v Willoughby (1841) 6 M & W 540 91
Froom v Butcher [1976] QB 286..139
Frost v Chief Constable of West Yorkshire Police
[1998] QB 254 ....35, 36

Giles v Walker (1890) 24 QBD 656 ....70, 72
Gillingham Borough Council v Medway (Chatham)
Dock Co [1993] QB 343 68
Glasgow Corporation v Muir [1943] AC 448 9
Glasgow Corporation v Taylor [1922] 1 AC 44 ....47, 48
Goldman v Hargreaves [1967] 1 AC 645..46
Goodwill v British Pregnancy Advisory Service
[1996] 2 All ER 161 42
Grant v Australian Knitting Mills [1936]
All ER Rep 209..91, 93
Green v Chelsea Waterworks Co (1894)
70 LT 547...70, 79
Greg v Scott [2005] UKHL 2; [2005] 2 WLR 268 22
Gwillam v West Hertfordshire National Health
Service Trust [2002] 3 WLR 1425 52

Hale v Jennings Bros [1948] 1 All ER 579 ....70, 76
Haley v London Electricity Board [1965] AC 778................................11
Halsey v Esso Petroleum Co Ltd [1961]
2 All ER 145 62
Hambrook v Stokes Bros [1925] 1 KB 141 31
Harrison v Duke of Rutland [1893] 1 QB 142 88
Haseldine v Daw & Sons Ltd [1941] 2 KB 343 ....47, 51
Hedley Bryne v Heller and Partners Ltd
[1964] AC 465 ....3, 40
Henderson v Merrett Syndicates [1994] 3 All ER 506................................43
Herd v Weardale Steel, Coal and Coke Co
[1915] AC 67 ....95, 106
Hickman v Maisey [1900] 1 QB 752 ....85, 89
Hill v Chief Constable of West Yorkshire
[1988] 2 All ER 238 7
Holbeck Hall Hotel Ltd v Scarborough
Borough Council [2000] 2 All ER 705..63
Hollywood Silver Fox Farm Ltd v Emmet
[1936] 2 KB 468 61
Home Office v Dorset Yacht Co Ltd [1970]
AC 1004 45
Hotson v East Berkshire Area Health Authority
[1987] 1 All ER 210 22
Hsu v Commissioner of Police for the Metropolis
[1997] 3 WLR 402...95, 106
Hughes v The Lord Advocate [1963] AC 837..28, 50

Hulton & Co v Jones [1910] AC 20 ....109, 111
Hunter and another v Canary Wharf [1997]
    AC 655; [1997] 2 All ER 426 ....58, 59, 76

Jobling v Associated Dairies Ltd [1982] AC 794 21
Jolley v London Borough of Sutton [2000]
    3 All ER 409 ....28, 50
Jones v Livox Quarries Ltd [1952] 2 QB 608 ....121, 133

Kaye v Robertson [1991] FSR 62 ....109, 119
Kelsen v Imperial Tobacco Co Ltd [1956] 2 QB 334 88
Kemsley v Foot [1952] AC 345 ....109, 116
Kennaway v Thompson [1981] 2 WLR 311 68
Knightley v Johns [1982] 1 All ER 851 25
Knupffer v London Express Newspapers Ltd [1944] AC 116 ....109, 114

Lane v Holloway [1968] 1 QB 379 ....95, 103
Latimer v AEC Ltd [1953] AC 643 12
Laws v Florinplace Ltd [1981] 1 All ER 659 60
Leakey v The National Trust [1980] QB 485 ....58, 64
Letang v Cooper [1965] 1 QB 232 ....95, 98
Lister v Hesley Hall Ltd [2001] 2 All ER 760;
    (2002) 65 MLE 270 ....121, 126, 127
Lister v Romford Ice & Cold Storage Ltd
    [1957] AC 555 127
Lloyd v Grace Smith & Co [1912] AC 716...127
Lonrho Ltd v Shell Petroleum Co Ltd (No 2)
    [1982] AC 173 ....121, 134
Lord v Pacific Steam Navigation Co Ltd,
    The Oropesa [1943] 1 All ER 211 24
Lord Bernstein of Leigh v Skyviews & General Ltd
    [1977] QB 479 ....85, 87

McGhee v National Coal Board [1973] 3 All ER 1008.............................17
McKew v Holland, Hannen & Cubitts (Scotland) Ltd
    [1969] 3 All ER 1621 ....3, 23
McLoughlin v O'Brian [1982] 2 All ER 298...32, 33
McQuaker v Goddard [1940] 1 KB 687 81
Marcic v Thames Water plc [2003] UKHL 66;
    [2003] 3 WLR 1603 ....58, 65
Mason v Levy Auto Parts of England [1967] 2 QB 530 ....70, 74
Meering v Graham White Aviation (1919) 122 LT 44 ....95, 105
Mersey Docks & Harbour Board v Coggins and Griffiths
    (Liverpool) Ltd [1947] AC 1..122
Miles v Forest Rock Granite Co (Leicestershire) Ltd
    (1918) 34 TLR 500, CA...72
Miller v Jackson [1977] QB 966 66
Mirvahedy v Henley [2003] UKHL 16; [2003] 2 AC 491 ....70, 83
Monson v Tussauds [1894] 1 QB 671...109, 110

Morgans v Launchbury [1973] AC 127 128
Murphy v Brentwood District Council [1991] 2 All ER 908 ....3, 6, 39
Musgrove v Pandelis [1919] 2 KB 43...73
Mutual Life and Citizens Assurance Co Ltd v Evatt
    [1971] AC 793 41

Nash v Sheen [1953] CLY 3726 100
Nettleship v Weston [1971] 2 QB 691 13
Nichols v Marsland (1876) 2 Ex D 1..137
North Glamorgan NHS Trust v Walters [2002]
    EWCA Civ 1792...36

Overseas Tankship (UK) Ltd v Morts Dock & Engineering
    Co, *The Wagon Mound* (No 1) [1961] AC 388 ....3, 26 , 29, 30

Page v Smith [1996] 3 All ER 272...3, 34
Pape v Cumbria County Council [1992] 3 All ER 211 130
Parker v British Airways Board [1982] QB 1004................................91, 92
Perera v Vandiyar [1953] 1 WLR 672..85, 86
Perry v Kendricks Transport Ltd [1956] 1 WLR 85 ....70, 79
Peters v Prince of Wales Theatre (Birmingham) Ltd
    [1943] KB 73 78
Phipps v Rochester Corporation [1955] 1 QB 450 ....47, 49
Poland v Parr [1927] 1 KB 236...121, 124
Polemis and Furness, Withy & Co, *Re* [1921] 3 KB 560 ....26, 27, 29

R v Ireland; R v Burstow [1998] AC 147, HL..................................95, 97
Ratcliffe v McConnell [1999] 1 WLR 670 ....47, 57
Read v Coker (1853) 13 CB 850...95, 96, 98
Read v Lyons [1947] AC 156..70, 74, 76
Ready Mixed Concrete (South East) Ltd v Minister of
    Pensions and National Insurance [1968] 2 QB 497 ....121, 123
Reeves v Metropolitan Police Commissioner
    [2000] 1 AC 360...7
Reilly v Merseyside Regional Health Authority
    (1994) 23 BMLR 26...3, 37
Revill v Newbery [1996] QB 567 138
Reynolds v Times Newspapers [2001] 2 AC 127 ....109, 117
Rickards v Lothian [1913] AC 263 ....70, 73
Rigby v Chief Constable of Northamptonshire
    [1985] 2 All ER 985...85, 90
Robert Addie & Sons (Collieries) Ltd v Dumbreck
    [1929] All ER 1...54
Robinson v Balmain New Ferry [1910] AC 295 105
Robinson v Kilvert (1889) 41 Ch D 88..58, 61
Roe v Minister of Health [1954] 2 QB 66.....................................9, 10
Roles v Nathan [1963] 1 WLR 1117..47, 50
Rose v Plenty [1976] 1 WLR 141 ....121, 124
Rylands v Fletcher (1868) LR 1 Exch 265; LR 3 HL 330..........70, 71, 75, 78

S (Adult: Refusal of Medical Treatment), *Re* [1992] 3 WLR 806 103
Sedleigh Denfield v O'Callaghan [1940] AC 880 ....58, 67
Sion v Hampstead Health Authority [1994] 5 Med LR 170 37
Smith v Baker [1891] AC 325 136
Smith v Eric S Bush [1990] 2 WLR 790 42
Smith v Leech Brain & Co Ltd [1961] 3 All ER 1159 29
Smith v Littlewoods Organisation Ltd [1987] 1 All ER 710 ....3, 44
Smolden v Whitworth and Nolan [1997] PIQR P133 13
Spartan Steel v Martin & Co (Contractors) Ltd [1973] 1 QB 27 39
St Helens Smelting Co v Tipping (1865) 11 HL Cas 642 ....58, 59
Stanley v Powell [1891] 1 QB 86..137
Staples v West Dorset District Council (1995) 93 LGR 536..................47, 53
Sturges v Bridgman (1879) 11 Ch D 852 ....58, 65
Sutherland v Hatton and Others [2002] EWCA Civ 76............121, 131, 132
Sutherland Shire Council v Heyman (1985) 60 ALR 1 5

T (an Adult) (Refusal of Medical Treatment),
    Re [1992] 3 WLR 782 101
Telnikoff v Matusevitch [1992] 4 All ER 817 115
Tetley and others v Chitty and others [1986] 1 All ER 663 64
Theaker v Richardson [1962] 1 WLR 151 ....109, 111
Thomas v National Union of Mineworkers [1986] 1 Ch 20.................95, 96
Tolley v Fry & Sons Ltd [1931] AC 333..109, 112
Tomlinson v Congleton Borough Council [2003] 1 AC 46 ....47, 55
Transco plc v Stockport Metropolitan Borough Council
    [2003] UKHL 61; [2003] 3 WLR 1467...77
Tremain v Pike [1969] 3 All ER 1303 27
Trotman v North Yorkshire County Council (1999) LGR 584 126
Tuberville v Savage (1669) 1 Mod Rep 3 ....95, 97
Tutin v Mary Chipperfield Promotions Ltd (1980)
    130 NLJ 807...70, 80
Twine v Beans Express [1946] 1 All ER 202 ....121, 125

Vernon v Boseley [1997] 1 All ER 577 38
Viasystems (Tyneside) Ltd v Thermal Transfer (Northern)
    Ltd [2005] EWCA Civ 1151 126
Victoria Railway Commissioners v Coultas
    (1888) 13 App Cas 222...30
Vizetelly v Mudie's Select Library Ltd [1900] 2 QB 170............................116
Vowles v Evans [2003] EWCA Civ 318; [2003] 1 WLR 1607 14

Wagner v International Railway Co (USA) 133
Wagon Mound, The, see Overseas Tankship (UK) Ltd v
    Morts Dock & Engineering Co, *The Wagon Mound*
Wainwright v Home Office [2003] UKHL 53;
    [2003] 3 WLR 1137..95, 107, 120
Walker v Northumberland County Council [1995] 1 All ER 737 130
Watt v Hertfordshire County Council [1954] 1 WLR 835..........................12
Westwood v The Post Office [1974] AC 1 56

Wheat v E Lacon & Co Ltd [1966] AC 552 ....47, 48
Wheeler v JJ Saunders Ltd [1996] Ch 19 ....58, 68
White v Blakemore [1972] 3 All ER 158..47, 53
White v Chief Constable of South Yorkshire [1999] 1 All ER 1 35
White v Jones [1995] 1 All ER 691 ....43, 44
Wilkinson v Downton [1897] 2 QB 57 ....95, 107, 108
Wilsher v Essex Area Health Authority [1988] 3 All ER 871 18
Wilson v Pringle [1987] 2 All ER 440..95, 99, 101
Wilson & Clyde Coal Co Ltd v English [1938] AC 57......................121, 129
Woodward v Hastings Corporation [1945] KB 174 52

Youssoupoff v MGM Pictures Ltd (1934) 50 TLR 581 110

Z and others v United Kingdom [2001] 2 FLR 612;
     (2001) EHRR 3 1

The Key Cases series is designed to give a clear understanding of important cases. This is useful when studying a new topic and invaluable as a revision aid.

Each case is broken down into fact and law. In addition, many cases are extended by the use of important extracts from the judgment or by comment or by highlighting problems. In some instances students are reminded that there is a link to other cases or material. If the link case is in another part of the same Key Cases book, the reference will be clearly shown. Some links will be to additional cases or materials that do not feature in the book.

To give a clear layout, symbols have been used at the start of each component of the case. The symbols are:

 Key Facts – These are the basic facts of the case.

 Key Law – This is the major principle of law in the case, the *ratio decidendi*.

 Key Judgment – This is an actual extract from a judgment made on the case.

 Key Comment – Influential or appropriate comments made on the case.

 Key Problem – Apparent inconsistencies or difficulties in the law.

 Key Link – This indicates other cases in the text which should be considered with this case.

The Key Link symbol alerts readers to links within the book and also to cases and other material, especially statutory provisions, which is not included.

At the start of each chapter there are mind maps highlighting the main cases and points of law. In addition, within most chapters, one or two of the most important cases are boxed to identify them and stress their importance.

Each Key Cases book can be used in conjunction with the Key Facts book on the same subject. Equally, they can be used as additional material to support any other textbook.

This Key Cases book on tort starts with cases on some general principles and then covers the main cases on negligence, occupiers' liability, nuisance, strict liability, trespass to land, torts concerning goods, trespass to the person, torts affecting reputation, employment-related torts and the general defences.

The law is stated as I believe it to be on 1st December 2005.

Chris Turner

CHAPTER 1

THE NATURE OF TORTIOUS LIABILITY

1.1 General principles of liability

HL **Bradford Corporation v Pickles** [1895] AC 587

The claimant supplied water to Bradford from sources that ran through underground channels beneath the defendant's land. The claimant alleged that, in an attempt to force it to buy his land, the defendant drained water from his land, causing the claimant's reservoir to empty. The claimant sought an injunction to prevent the defendant from drawing water from his land but this was denied.

The defendant's motive for drawing water from his land was held to be irrelevant, even if it was through malice. The defendant was legitimately exercising property rights in extracting water from his land. The claimant only had rights to the water once it reached its land and the injunction was denied.

1.2 Human rights and tort

CHR **Z and others v United Kingdom** [2001] 2 FLR 612; [2001] EHRR 3

A family of young children first came to the attention of a Social Services Department in 1987. The local authority failed to apply for a care order until 1992. In the meantime, neighbours, teachers, police, doctors and health visitors all expressed concern about the children's welfare. A psychiatrist who examined the children in 1993 reported that it was the worst case of neglect and emotional abuse that she had ever seen. The Official Solicitor brought an action for negligence against the local authority, arguing that the children had suffered long-term damage that could have been avoided if the council had acted promptly. The action failed in the House of Lords and was taken to the European Court of Human Rights.

The House of Lords held that it would not be just or reasonable to impose a duty since it would cut across the council's other statutory duties, removing resources that could otherwise be used for child protection. The Children Act 1989 was for public benefit generally, not private rights. The European Court of Human Rights accepted that the children were subjected to inhuman and degrading treatment contrary to Art 3, denied a fair trial contrary to Art 6, and refused an effective remedy contrary to Art 13.

The result of this ruling is that English courts will have to rethink the apparent blanket immunity from liability that they have in the past been prepared to extend to public bodies in negligence actions.

CHAPTER 2

NEGLIGENCE

Duty of care
Caparo v Dickman (1990)
Must show foreseeability of harm, proximity and fair just and reasonable to impose a duty
Breach of duty
Blyth v Birmingham Waterworks (1856)
Standard is that of the reasonable man
Bolton v Stone (1951)
Should take into account factors such as foreseeability of harm, the magnitude of risk, practicality of precautions etc
Bolam v Friern Hospital Management Committee (1957)
Standard of doctors is that of a competent body of professional opinion
Causation
Barnett v Chelsea & Kensington Hospital (1969)
Must show damage would not have occurred 'but for' defendant's breach
Fairchild v Glenhaven (2002)
But where there are multiple causes a material contribution may be sufficient
The Wagon Mound (1961)
The damage must be foreseeable or is too remote
McKew v Holland, Hannen & Cubitts (1969)
The chain of causation may be broken by a *'novus actus interveniens'*

→ Negligence ←

Nervous shock
Reilly v Merseyside Regional Health Authority (1994)
Must be a recognised psychiatric illness caused by a single traumatic event
Page v Smith (1996)
Primary victims are those present at the scene and at risk of some harm
Alcock v Chief Constable of South Yorkshire (1992)
Secondary victims must show close tie of love and affection with primary victim and be present at scene or immediate aftermath, and witness event with own unaided senses

Omissions
Smith v Littlewoods (1987)
Liability for failure to act only if there is a duty to act

Economic loss
Murphy v Brentwood District Council (1991)
Generally no liability for pure economic loss caused by negligent actions
Hedley Byrne v Heller & Partners (1964)
But can be for economic loss caused by negligently made statements if made by a person with expertise in the matter who knows that the advice is relied on

2.1 Duty of care

HL **Donoghue v Stevenson**
[1932] AC 562

The claimant claimed to suffer shock and gastro-enteritis after drinking ginger beer from an opaque bottle out of which a decomposing snail had fallen when the dregs were poured. A friend had bought her the drink and so the claimant could not sue in contract. She was owed a duty of care by the manufacturer despite the fact that she had no contractual relationship.

A manufacturer owes a duty of care towards consumers or users of his products not to cause them harm (often referred to as the 'narrow *ratio*' of the case).

Lord Atkin also identified the means of establishing the existence of a duty of care (the 'neighbour principle'):

'You must take reasonable care to avoid acts or omissions which you can reasonably foresee would be likely to injure your neighbour. Who then in law is my neighbour? … persons who are so closely and directly affected by my act that I ought reasonably to have them in my contemplation as being affected so when I am directing my mind to the acts or omissions in question'.

Lord Atkin's judgment also exploded the so-called 'privity fallacy' and is credited with creating a separate tort of negligence. Negligence can be proved by showing:

- the existence of a duty of care owed to the claimant by the defendant;
- a breach of that duty by the defendant falling below the appropriate standard of care;
- damage caused by the defendant's breach of duty that was not too remote a consequence of the breach, i.e. that was a foreseeable consequence of the breach.

HL **Anns v Merton London Borough Council [1978] AC 728**

A local authority had failed to ensure that building work complied with the plans, as a result of which the building had inadequate foundations. The claimant, a tenant who had leased the property after it had changed hands many times, claimed that the damage to the property threatened health and safety, and sued successfully.

Lord Wilberforce, on policy grounds, held that there was sufficient proximity between the authority and the tenant to enable a duty to be owed and there was no reason not to impose the duty.

In *Curran v Northern Ireland Co-ownership Housing Association Ltd* 1987 AC 718 Lord Bridge approved the judgment of Brennan J in the High Court of Australia in *Sutherland Shire Council v Heyman* 1985 60 ALR 1, where he argued that it was 'preferable that the law should develop novel categories of negligence incrementally and by analogy with established categories, rather than by a massive extension of a prima facie duty of care restrained only by indefinable "considerations which ought to negative or to reduce or limit the scope of the duty or the class of the person to whom it is owed".' The 'Anns' test was overruled in *Murphy v Brentwood District Council* [1991] 2 All ER 908 as a result.

HL **Caparo Industries plc v Dickman** [1990] 1 All ER 568

Shareholders in a company bought more shares and then made a successful take-over bid for the company after studying the audited accounts prepared by the defendants. They later regretted the move and sued the auditors, claiming that they had relied on accounts which had shown a sizeable surplus rather than the deficit that was in fact the case. Their case failed.

The House of Lords held that the auditors owed no duty of care to the claimants since company accounts are not prepared for the purposes of people taking over a company and cannot then be relied on by them for such purposes. The court also developed the three-stage test for determining when a duty of care is owed:

- Firstly, it should be considered whether the consequences of the defendant's behaviour were reasonably foreseeable.
- Secondly, the court should consider whether there is sufficient legal proximity between the parties for a duty to be imposed.
- Lastly, the court should ask whether or not it is fair, just and reasonable in all the circumstances to impose a duty of care.

HL | Hill v Chief Constable of West Yorkshire
[1988] 2 All ER 238

The mother of the final victim of the Yorkshire Ripper claimed against the police for their careless and ineffective handling of the case, arguing that her daughter would not have died but for the negligence in the police investigation. The claim failed.

The court held that there was insufficient proximity between the police and the public for a duty to be imposed to protect individual members of the public from specific crimes.

This was an obvious policy decision. However, even under the three-part test it would be considered unfair, unjust and unreasonable to impose such a duty on the police.

Reeves v Metropolitan Police Commissioner [2000] 1 AC 360 (where police owed a duty to a known suicide risk while he was in custody and could not rely on *volenti* when he did commit suicide).

2.2 Breach of the duty of care

2.2.1 The standard of care and the 'reasonable man' test

Exch
Div **Blyth v Proprietors of the Birmingham Waterworks**
(1856) 11 Exch 781

A water main was laid with a 'fire plug', a wooden plug in the main that would allow water to flow through a cast iron tube up to the street when necessary. The plug became loose in severe frost and water flooded the claimant's house because the cast iron tube was blocked with ice. The frost was beyond normal expectation.

The court held that the defendants had done all they reasonably could have done to prevent the damage, so there was no liability.

Alderson B stated: 'Negligence is the omission to do something which a reasonable man, guided upon those considerations which ordinarily regulate human affairs, would do, or doing something which a prudent and reasonable man would not do.'

HL **Glasgow Corporation v Muir** [1943] AC 448

A tea urn was being carried through a narrow passage in the defendant's premises where small children were buying ice creams. Some children were scalded when the urn was dropped. Their claim for damages failed.

The court assessed liability by using the 'reasonable man' test and held that the damage was not foreseeable and not a risk that the defendant should have guarded against.

MacMillan LJ explained the objective test:
'The standard of foresight of the reasonable man is an impersonal test ... independent of the idiosyncrasies of the particular person whose conduct is in question. Some persons are by nature unduly timorous and imagine every path beset by lions; others, of more robust temperament, fail to foresee or nonchalantly disregard even the most obvious dangers. The reasonable man is presumed to be free from both over-apprehension and from over-confidence.'

2.2.2 Principles in determining the standard of care

CA **Roe v Minister of Health** [1954] 2 QB 66

Two patients became paralysed after being injected with nupercaine, a spinal anaesthetic. The nupercaine was sealed in glass ampoules which were stored in a sterilising fluid, phenol. Evidence at the trial showed that the phenol solution had entered the anaesthetic through hairline cracks in the ampoules, contaminating it and causing the paralysis. The claims for damages failed.

There was no liability because such an event had not previously occurred and was unforeseeable as a result.

As McBride and Bagshaw point out (*Tort Law* (2nd ed, Pearson Publishing, 2005) pp 38–40):
'if ... the function of tort law is to determine when someone who has suffered loss at another's hands [is] entitled to sue ... you will think that tort law failed the patients in *Roe* ... the truth is more complicated ... the patients could not establish that the hospital had committed a civil wrong ... tort law imposed a duty on the hospital to treat the patients with reasonable ... care and skill; but the hospital fully discharged that duty ... No one could have foreseen that treating the patients in the way they were treated would expose them to the risk of paralysis'.

HL **Bolton v Stone [1951] AC 850**

Miss Stone was standing on a pavement by a cricket ground when she was hit by a cricket ball that was hit out of the ground. She was standing 100 yards from where the batsman had struck the ball. The batsman was 78 yards from a 17-foot-high fence over which the ball had been struck. It was also shown that balls had only been struck out of the ground six times in 28 years. The claimant's action in negligence failed.

It was held that the likelihood of harm was extremely low and that the cricket ground had done everything reasonably possible to avoid risks of people being hit. There was no breach of duty.

Lord Radcliffe identified the connection with the 'reasonable man' test:
'unless there has been something which a reasonable man would blame as falling beneath the standard of conduct that he would set for himself … there has been no breach of legal duty.'

HL **Haley v London Electricity Board** [1965] AC 778

The defendant's workmen were digging a hole along a pavement and had left a hammer propped up on the pavement to warn passers-by of the presence of the hole. The claimant was a blind man who was passing and whose stick failed to touch the hammer so that he tripped over the hammer and fell heavily, becoming deaf as a result. His claim in negligence was successful.

The court held that there was a sufficiently large proportion of blind people in the community for the risk of harm to be great. The cost of the necessary precautions to protect blind people would have been very low. The defendants were liable for negligence.

CA Watt v Hertfordshire County Council [1954] 1 WLR 835

A woman was trapped under a heavy vehicle and seriously injured. The fire service called to free her had a special jack for use in such circumstances. This would normally be transported securely in a special vehicle, but this was in use elsewhere. The jack was taken unsecured in another vehicle because of the emergency. When the driver was forced to brake sharply the jack moved, injuring one of the firemen. His claim for damages was unsuccessful.

The court held that there was no negligence because the situation was an emergency; those in charge had to balance the nature of the risk against the importance of the emergency. The risk was justified in the circumstances.

HL Latimer v AEC Ltd [1953] AC 643

A factory floor became flooded during a torrential rainstorm. The water mixed with oil and grease on the floor so that the surface was slippery and dangerous. Once the water was cleared, sawdust was spread over the floor to make it safe to walk on. There was not enough to cover the whole floor and the claimant slipped on an oily patch and injured his ankle. His action for damages failed.

The House of Lords held that everything reasonable and practicable had been done in the circumstances to avoid risk of harm and, balancing out the possible risks, it was unreasonable to expect the factory to be closed. There was no negligence.

CA Nettleship v Weston [1971] 2 QB 691

A learner driver on her third lesson crashed into a lamppost and injured her instructor. The question for the court was whether a lower standard of care should be expected of her because she was a learner driver. She was still found liable.

The Court of Appeal found that she was liable despite being a learner driver since exactly the same standard of skill was expected of her as would be expected of a competent driver.

Lord Denning stated that the law demands from a learner driver 'the same standard of care as of any other driver. The learner driver may be doing his best, but his incompetent best is not good enough. He must drive in as good a manner as a driver of skill, experience and care ... who makes no errors of judgment ...'.

It was also identified that this is probably to do with the requirement of compulsory motoring insurance so that the degree of risk associated with the particular type of driver can be reflected in the insurance premium they have to pay.

CA Smolden v Whitworth and Nolan [1997] PIQR P133

In a Colts rugby match, involving players under 19 years of age, the referee was approached by the coach of one team about repeated collapsing of the scrum by players from the other team. The referee did not control the scrums properly and the 17-year-old claimant was seriously injured, leading to paralysis, when the scrum was again collapsed. The claim for damages, arguing that the referee had failed to match the appropriate standard of care, succeeded.

The Court of Appeal agreed that the referee had fallen below the standard of care that he owed to the players. This was because rules relating to scrums had been introduced for Colts' games specifically to protect young players from spinal injury which was a foreseeable risk and these rules therefore imposed a higher standard of care on the referees in such games.

Vowles v Evans [2003] EWCA Civ 318; [2003] 1 WLR 1607, where it was held that a rugby referee owes a duty of care to the players to enforce the rules of the game because the players depended on these rules for avoiding injury.

2.2.3 The standard of care owed by professionals

QBD | **Bolam v Friern Hospital Management Committee**
[1957] 2 All ER 118

The claimant suffered from depression and consented to undergo electro-convulsive therapy, a practice which can cause severe muscular spasms. The doctor giving the treatment failed to provide relaxant drugs or any means of restraint and the claimant suffered a fractured pelvis. The claimant maintained that the procedure carried out in this way was negligent but he failed in his action for damages.

The court accepted evidence showing that doctors at the time were divided on whether or not to use relaxant drugs during the procedure. The defendant was not negligent because he engaged in a procedure accepted by a competent body of medical practitioners skilled in the particular field.

McNair J established that a different standard of care was appropriate to doctors:

'In the ordinary case which does not involve any special skill ... negligence ... means a failure to do some act which a reasonable man in the circumstances would do, or the doing of some act which a reasonable man in the circumstances would not do ... But where you get a situation which involves the use of some special skill or competence, then the test as to whether there has been negligence or not is not the test of the man on the top of a Clapham omnibus, because he has not got this skill ... The test is the standard of the ordinary skilled man exercising and professing to have that special skill ... Putting it the other way round, a doctor is not negligent, if he is acting in accordance with such a practice, merely because there is a body of opinion that takes a contrary view.'

Brazier and Miola (in 'Bye-bye *Bolam*: A medical Litigation Revolution?' (2000) *8 Med Law Review* (Spring), pp 85–114) argue that 'Many academic commentators and organisations campaigning for victims of medical accidents perceive [that] the *Bolam* test ... has been used by the courts to abdicate responsibility for defining and enforcing patient rights.'

HL Bolitho v City and Hackney Health Authority
[1998] AC 232

A two-year-old boy was in hospital being treated for croup. His airwaves became blocked and, despite the requests of the nurses, the doctor on call failed to attend. The boy suffered a cardiac arrest and brain damage as a result. This could have been avoided if a doctor had intubated the boy and cleared the obstruction. The hospital admitted that the doctor was negligent in failing to attend, but claimed that it was not liable because the doctor would not have intubated even if she had attended, so there would have been no difference in the outcome, and that not intubating was acceptable medical practice.

The case was ultimately decided on causation but the House rejected the view that because certain medical opinion would accept the practice of a doctor as reasonable and responsible it was bound to accept that merely because of *Bolam*.

Lord Browne-Wilkinson suggested that
'... if, in a rare case, it can be demonstrated that the professional opinion is not capable of withstanding logical analysis, the judge is entitled to hold that the body of opinion is not reasonable or responsible'

but added

'It is only where a judge can be satisfied that the body of expert opinion cannot be logically supported at all that such opinion will not provide the bench mark by reference to which the defendant's conduct falls to be assessed'.

The House of Lords, taking up the criticism of *Bolam* expressed by many academic commentators, seems to be suggesting that there are circumstances where the test would not be followed. The problem is that it gives no examples of what circumstances this would occur in.

2.3 Causation and remoteness of damage

2.3.1 Causation in fact

QBD **Barnett v Chelsea & Kensington Hospital Management Committee** [1969] 1 QB 428

The claimant went to the casualty ward of the hospital at around 5 am on the morning of New Year's Day, complaining of vomiting and stomach pains after drinking tea. The doctor on duty, in clear breach of his duty, refused to examine him and told him to see his own doctor in the morning. The claimant later died of arsenic poisoning. It was shown that the man would have died even with treatment.

On a straightforward application of the 'but for' test the failure to treat was not the factual cause of death so there was no liability.

HL **McGhee v National Coal Board** [1973] 3 All ER 1008

The claimant worked in a brick kiln and contracted dermatitis, one possible cause being the brick dust to which he was exposed. The claimant argued a breach of duty because the employer did not provide washing facilities.

The Board was held liable on the basis that it 'materially increased the risk' of the claimant contracting the disease because of its failure to provide washing facilities, even though it could not be shown that he would have avoided the disease if facilities had been in place.

As the employer was negligent in failing to provide basic health and safety the court felt that it should have the burden of disproving the causal link. The test is more advantageous to a claimant than the basic 'but for' test but potentially unfair on the defendant.

HL **Wilsher v Essex Area Health Authority** [1988] 3 All ER 871

After a difficult delivery, a baby was mistakenly given too much oxygen by the doctor. The baby suffered retrolental fibroplasias, resulting in blindness. The House of Lords accepted evidence that excess oxygen was just one of six possible causes of the condition and dismissed the claim.

The House of Lords applied the 'but for' test rigidly. Since the doctor's error was one of six possible causes the blindness could not be said to fall squarely within the risk created by the defendants.

HL **Fairchild v Glenhaven Funeral Services Ltd and others; Fox v Spousal (Midlands) Ltd; Matthews v Associated Portland Cement Manufacturers (1978) Ltd and another**
[2002] UKHL 22; [2002] 3 WLR 89

Three joined appeals involved employees who had contracted mesothelioma through prolonged exposure to asbestos dust with a number of different employers. It is currently scientifically uncertain whether inhaling a single fibre or inhalation of many fibres causes the disease, so it was impossible to say accurately which employer caused the disease. Nevertheless, the claims succeeded against the specific employers who were sued.

The House of Lords held that, since greater exposure to the dust means that the chances of contracting the disease are greater, then each employer has a duty to take reasonable care to prevent employees from inhaling the dust and that any of the employers could be liable because they had all materially contributed to the risk of harm. Since the claimants suffered the very injuries that the defendants were supposed to guard against the House was prepared to impose liability on all employers. Because the employers never argued that they should only be liable for a proportion of the damages each employer should be liable to compensate its employee in full, even though the employee may have inhaled more fibres while working for another employee.

The House accepted that sufferers of diseases such as mesothelioma, while inevitably deserving of compensation, are unable to satisfy the normal tests for causation because they are unable to point to a single party who is responsible. The court was prepared to accept the possibility of a claim for three connected reasons:

- Because claimants could only not satisfy the normal tests for causation because of the current state of medical knowledge, although there is no doubt that exposure to asbestos fibres in whatever volume is the cause of the disease.
- As a result, it was fairer to give the defendants the burden of proving that their negligence could not be the actual cause.
- If this approach was not taken then it would be almost impossible to make successful claims for the disease so the employer's duty of care would be made meaningless.

HL **Baker v Willoughby [1970] AC 467**

Through the defendant's negligent driving the claimant suffered a permanent disability in his leg which meant that he had to take work on a lower income. Some time later, he was shot in the same leg by an armed robber which meant that his leg then had to be amputated. The House of Lords rejected the defendant's claim that he was only liable for damages up to the point of the amputation.

The court identified that the loss of earnings was a permanent result of the original injury and unaffected by the amputation.

Lord Reid explained:
'A man is not compensated for the physical injury; he is compensated for the loss which he suffers as a result .... His loss is not in having a stiff leg; it is in his inability to lead a full life ... to enjoy those amenities which depend on freedom of movement and ... to earn as much as he used to earn or could have earned if there had been no accident. In this case the second injury did not diminish any of these.'

HL **Jobling v Associated Dairies Ltd** [1982] AC 794

In 1973, as a result of his employer's negligence, the claimant slipped on the floor of a refrigerator in the butcher's shop where he worked and injured his back, losing 50 per cent of his earning capacity as a result. In 1976 he developed spondylotic myelopathy, a back disorder unrelated to the fall, which meant he could not work at all. The court held that the defendant employer was liable for damages only up to when the condition developed in 1976.

The House held that, since the condition would have occurred anyway, then the defendant's negligence had only caused the loss of earnings prior to that point. Any later loss of earnings would have occurred anyway, despite the defendant's negligence.

The court, while not overruling *Baker*, was nevertheless very critical of the case.

HL | **Greg v Scott [2005] UKHL 2; [2005] 2 WLR 268**

The claimant consulted his GP about a lump under his arm.
The doctor diagnosed fatty tissue and failed to send the
claimant to hospital for any further tests, which he should
have done because cancer was a foreseeable possibility. Nine
months later it was discovered that the lump was a cancer.
Medical evidence was accepted that the claimant would have
had a 42 per cent chance of being alive and cancer free in 10
years if the cancer had been diagnosed and treated after the
first visit. This had reduced to a 25 per cent chance by the
time the nine months had passed. The claimant unsuccessfully
sought damages for the reduction in his prospects of cure and
life expectancy.

The House held that it would be to develop the law in a way
that was inappropriate to allow a claim for a proportion of
what would have been awarded if the defendant had been
proved to have been the cause of the claimant's premature
death. In fact all that could be proved was a loss of a chance of
full recovery and the law does not accept this as a basis for
showing causation.

Hotson v East Berkshire Area Health Authority [1987] 1 All ER 210

HL | **Chester v Ashfar [2004] UKHL 41; [2005] 1 AC 134**

The defendant neurosurgeon failed to warn the claimant of a
1–2 per cent risk of partial paralysis from the procedure, and
which she in fact suffered. The claimant succeeded in her

claim for damages because the court accepted that she had proved that if she had been properly informed she would not have undergone the surgery.

The House held that the claimant could not satisfy the normal 'but for' test, since it was possible that she may have consented to the operation at a future date. However, the court felt that justice required that in order to give practical force to a doctor's legal duty to warn a patient of the risks involved in surgery it should treat the injury as though it had been caused by the defendant's breach.

2.3.2 *Novus actus interveniens*

HL **McKew v Holland & Hannen & Cubitts (Scotland) Ltd**
[1969] 3 All ER 1621

The claimant suffered an injury to his leg caused by the defendants' negligence. For some time after the event, he suffered from a condition which meant that his leg frequently gave way. While in this condition he tried to climb down a steep flight of steps with no handrail, without any help and while carrying his daughter. He fell when his leg gave way and suffered further serious injuries. The defendants were not held liable for this further injury.

The court held that the defendants were not liable for this fall. The claimant's act was a *novus actus interveniens*. He was fully aware of the weakness in his leg and his behaviour was unreasonable.

Lord Reid explained:
'if the injured man acts unreasonably he cannot hold the defender liable for injury caused by his own unreasonable conduct. His unreasonable conduct is *novus actus interveniens*. The chain of causation has been broken and what follows must be regarded as being caused by his own conduct.'

➡

Lord v Pacific Steam Navigation Co. Ltd (The Oropesa) [1943] 1 All ER 211 where there was no *novus actus* because the claimant's behaviour was entirely reasonable in the circumstances.

HL | **Carslogie Steamship Co. v Royal Norwegian Government [1952] AC 292**

The claimant's ship was damaged in a collision with the defendant's ship through the defendant's negligence. Following a delay for repairs, the ship embarked on a voyage to a different destination, during which it suffered further damage caused by an exceptionally heavy storm. The claimant was not able to gain damages from the defendant for this extra damage.

The House accepted that the extra damage was caused by the storm which was a break in the chain of causation. It would have been unfair to fix the defendant with liability for the full extent of the damage. The storm damage was not a consequence of the collision but was a quite separate occurrence.

CA Knightley v Johns [1982] 1 All ER 851

The defendant, through negligent driving, crashed and blocked a tunnel. The police officer in charge at the scene sent a police motorcyclist back against the flow of traffic to block off the tunnel at the other end, in order to prevent further accidents. The police officer was injured when he collided with an oncoming car while rounding a bend. The defendant was not held liable for the police officer's injuries.

The court held that the defendant could not be said to have caused this injury. It was the fault of the senior police officer whose ill-considered action broke the chain of causation and was a *novus actus interveniens*.

Stephenson LJ made a quite significant comment in suggesting that 'Negligent conduct is more likely to break the chain of causation than conduct which is not.'

There is a clear problem for the claimant where the chain of conduct is broken by the act of a third party. If that act is not negligent then the claimant can receive no compensation for the extra harm suffered.

2.3.3 Remoteness of damage

PC **Overseas Tankship (UK) Ltd v Morts Dock & Engineering Co. (The Wagon Mound (No 1))** [1961] AC 388

As a result of the defendant's negligence, oil leaked into Sydney Harbour from its tanker. The oil floated on the water to the claimant's wharf. Welding was taking place in the wharf and the claimant's manager enquired whether there was a risk of the oil igniting. This was considered unlikely since the oil had an extremely high flash point. The welder continued and sparks ignited oil-soaked wadding and set fire to ships being repaired in the wharf. The oil also caused fouling to the wharf. The trial judge had held that since some damage, the fouling, was foreseeable, the defendants were also liable for the fire damage which was a direct consequence of its breach of duty in allowing the spillage. The Privy Council reversed this decision and disallowed damages for the fire damage.

The court held that the defendant could not be liable for the fire damage as it was too remote a consequence of the breach of duty. The true test should be based on reasonable foreseeability and, because of the unlikelihood of the oil igniting; the fire damage was not foreseeable to a reasonable man.

Viscount Simonds explained why the court rejected the former test of direct and natural consequences from *Re Polemis*:
'if it is asked why a man should be responsible for the natural or necessary or probable consequences of his act the answer is that it is not because they are natural or necessary or probable, but because, since they have this quality, it is judged by the standard of the reasonable man that he ought to have foreseen them.'

Re Polemis and Furness, Withy & Co. [1921] 3 KB 560

QBD **Tremain v Pike [1969] 3 All ER 1303**

The claimant was a herdsman who contracted Weil's Disease on his employer's farm which was infested with rats. This disease is very rare and can only be contracted through direct contact with rats' urine. The claimant argued that this did happen when he handled hay and washed in water that was contaminated with rats' urine. His claim failed.

The court accepted that the defendant had negligently let the rat population on his farm grow too high, so that there was risk of injury from rats. Nevertheless, the court held that the defendant was not liable since the court considered that the disease was too rare in humans and so was unforeseeable.

Payne J suggested that the disease was 'entirely different in kind from the effect of a rat bite or food poisoning'.

This is a very narrow view of foreseeability, particularly in view of the level to which the claimant was exposed to the rat urine. If injury from the rats was foreseeable then surely injury from the exposure to the urine was an equally foreseeable cause of harm.

HL Hughes v The Lord Advocate [1963] AC 837

Post Office employees dug a hole in the road and left a manhole uncovered inside a tent and then left the tent unattended. They also left four lit paraffin lamps at the corners of the tent at night as a warning and to avoid people falling in the hole. A boy entered the tent with one of the lamps and when it fell into the hole an explosion caused the boy to suffer burns. The boy's claim succeeded.

The House accepted that the precise circumstances in which the injury occurred were quite remote. However, some fire-related damage was a foreseeable consequence of leaving the scene unattended and so it held the defendants liable. Providing damage of the general kind was foreseeable, then this was sufficient.

This is a much broader and, from the claimant's perspective, a much more generous view of foreseeability.

Jolley v London Borough of Sutton [2000] 3 All ER 409:
see p50

CA Doughty v Turner Manufacturing Co. Ltd [1964] 1 QB 518

The cover on a tank of heated sodium cyanide was improperly secured so that it slid into the liquid in the tank while the claimant was working by it. The cover was made of asbestos and an explosion caused by the mixing of the chemicals and the asbestos badly burned the claimant. The claim for personal injury failed.

The Court of Appeal accepted that it was previously unknown that there would be such a chemical reaction. Applying *Wagon Mound* principles, the chemical reaction was thus unforeseeable and the damage was too remote to impose liability on the defendants.

This is a narrow view of the foreseeable circumstances in which an injury might occur. It seems foreseeable that injury of some type could occur if the lid fell into the chemical while the workman was by it. Interestingly, the Court of Appeal chose to apply persuasive precedent from the Privy Council in *The Wagon Mound* rather than its own previous precedent in *Re Polemis*.

QBD **Smith v Leech Brain & Co. Ltd** [1961] 3 All ER 1159

The claimant suffered a burnt lip as a result of being splashed by molten metal while at work, because of his employer's negligence. The burn ulcerated and activated a cancer from which he died three years later. He received full damages rather than just for the burn.

The court held that even though the death from cancer was an immediately foreseeable consequence of the negligence some form of injury clearly was and the defendants were held liable as a result. While it was accepted that his lip had actually been in a pre-malignant state at the time of the burn, some form of harm from the burn was foreseeable and the court rejected the argument that *Wagon Mound* principles prevented operation of the 'thin skull' rule.

This operates as an exception to the test of reasonable foreseeability. Where the 'thin skull' rule is applicable the test is still one of direct and natural consequences.

2.4 Nervous shock

PC | **Victoria Railway Commissioners v Coultas**
(1888) 13 App Cas 222

The claimant suffered no physical injury but claimed to suffer psychiatric injury when involved in a train crash.

The claim was refused because there was insufficient medical understanding of the nature of psychiatric injury at that time and there was no evidence of physical injury.

Claims for nervous shock were originally rejected not just because of the lack of understanding of psychiatric injury, but also because of the 'floodgates' argument. The judge feared that allowing the claim would open up a 'wide field of imaginary claims'.

KB Dulieu v White & Sons [1901] 2 KB 669

The claimant was the pregnant wife of a publican. She suffered nervous shock and her baby was born prematurely after a horse and van that had been negligently driven burst through the window of the pub where she was washing glasses. Her claim was successful even though she had suffered no physical injury.

The court held that the defendant was liable because the claimant was within the zone of impact of physical injury and some damage was therefore foreseeable. Kennedy J devised the test for claiming damages for psychiatric injury (to become known as the 'Kennedy' test: a claimant might recover damages if the claimant feared real and immediate danger to himself as a result of the sudden shock.

Kennedy J stated that: 'Shock, when it operates through the mind, must be a shock which arises from a reasonable fear of immediate personal injury to oneself.'

CA Hambrook v Stokes Bros [1925] 1 KB 141

A woman saw a runaway lorry going downhill towards where she had left her three children. She then heard that there had indeed been an accident involving a child. She suffered nervous shock and died.

The court extended claims for nervous shock to include those within the area of shock, i.e. those who while not in danger themselves feared for the safety of somebody who was.

The court distinguished the 'Kennedy' test. The judge considered that it would be unfair not to compensate a mother who had feared for the safety of her children when she could have claimed if she only feared for her own safety.

HL **Bourhill v Young** [1943] AC 92

A pregnant Edinburgh fishwife claimed to have suffered nervous shock after getting off a tram, hearing the impact of a crash involving a motorcyclist, and later seeing his blood on the road. She then gave birth to a stillborn child. Her claim failed.

The House of Lords held that, as a stranger to the motorcyclist, she was outside of the area of foreseeable shock. This then identifies the law on nervous shock in relation to bystanders. If they are not within the zone of danger and have no relationship with the primary victim then the damage they suffer is not foreseeable.

HL **McLoughlin v O'Brian** [1982] 2 All ER 298

A woman was summoned to a hospital about an hour after her children and husband were involved in a car crash. One child was dead, two were badly injured, all were in shock and they had not yet been cleaned up. She suffered nervous shock as a result and her claim succeeded.

The House of Lords held that since the relationship was sufficiently close and the woman was present at the 'immediate aftermath' she could claim. Lord Wilberforce identified a three-part test for secondary victims that was approved later in *Alcock*.

HL | **Alcock v Chief Constable of South Yorkshire**
[1992] 4 All ER 907

At the start of a football match police allowed a large crowd of supporters into a caged pen as the result of which 95 people in the stand suffered crush injuries and were killed. Since the match was being televised much of the disaster was shown on live TV. A number of claims for nervous shock were made. These varied between those present or not present at the scene, those with close family ties to the dead and those who were merely friends. The House of Lords refused all of the claims.

The House of Lords held that none of the claimants identified the factors that must be proved in order to make a successful claim as a secondary victim:

- The proximity in time and space to the negligent incident – the claimant must have been present at the scene or its immediate aftermath (limited to two hours following *McLoughlin*).

- The proximity of the relationship with a party who was a victim of the incident – the claimant must have a close tie of love and affection with a primary victim.
- The cause of the nervous shock – the claimant must show that he suffered nervous shock as a result of witnessing or hearing the horrifying event or its immediate aftermath.

The development of the law on secondary victims has been to develop controls based on public policy that limit the potential for a successful claim, the justification being the 'floodgates' argument. Claims were denied here even though the relationship with the primary victim was a family one. It is also possible that the proximity to and the gruesomeness of the incident makes it foreseeable that a bystander could suffer psychiatric injury in which case there is a contradiction with the reasoning for granting remedies to primary victims and many bystanders are being unfairly denied a remedy.

HL **Page v Smith [1996] 3 All ER 272**

Page was involved in a car accident caused by the defendant's negligence. He suffered no physical injury but did suffer a recurrence of 'chronic fatigue syndrome' (ME) from which he had suffered before. He recovered damages for nervous shock.

The House of Lords held that: firstly the illness in question was a recognised psychiatric injury; secondly that Page was indeed a genuine primary victim (present at the scene and at risk of foreseeable physical injury); thirdly that the 'thin skull' rule applied and that it did not matter that the single traumatic event led to injury that Page was more likely to suffer because of a pre-existing condition.

The situation for primary victims differs from that of secondary victims. The 'thin skull' rule applies to primary victims but a secondary victim would be expected to show 'reasonable phlegm and fortitude' – so a secondary victim with Page's condition would be unable to claim.

HL
White v Chief Constable of South Yorkshire
[1999] 1 All ER 1

Police officers who were present at the Hillsborough disaster as rescuers claimed to have suffered post-traumatic stress disorder. Their claim succeeded in the Court of Appeal as *Frost*. The House of Lords rejected their claim.

The House of Lords held that no claim was possible since the police officers could not be classed as primary victims since they were never in any danger. The Lords also identified that there is no longer any presumption that a rescuer is a primary victim. A rescuer can only claim if he can show that he was at risk of foreseeable physical injury, and is therefore a genuine primary victim.

The Law Lords were also worried about the effect on public opinion if they awarded damages to police officers from

Hillsborough when all the relatives of the dead had been denied claims.

Frost v Chief Constable of West Yorkshire Police [1998] QB 254

North Glamorgan NHS Trust v Walters
[2002] EWCA Civ 1792

Doctors negligently failed to diagnose that a tiny baby required a liver transplant, despite reassuring his mother that he would survive. He then suffered a major fit and both were taken to a London hospital for the child to have a liver transplant. On arrival it was discovered that he had irreversible and severe brain damage. The life support system was switched off and the baby died minutes later in his mother's arms, the whole episode lasting 36 hours. The mother claimed successfully for pathological grief. The defendants appealed on the grounds that the psychiatric injury was not brought about as a result of witnessing a single shocking event but the Court of Appeal rejected this argument.

The Court of Appeal held that the whole period from when the baby suffered the fit to when it died was 'a single horrifying event' and was part of a continuous chain of events.

The result seems to conflict quite sharply with the principle of single shocking event and the use of the 'immediate aftermath' test from *Alcock*. The Court of Appeal did in fact though distinguish from those cases where there is a slow realisation of the consequences of the shocking event.

Sion v Hampstead Health Authority
[1994] 5 Med LR 170

A father suffered psychiatric injury after watching his son over the space of 14 days gradually deteriorate and then die, when there was the possibility of the death resulting from medical negligence. He was unsuccessful because the psychiatric injury was not the result of the sudden appreciation of a single traumatic event.

Nervous shock must result from a single traumatic event. There is no claim for an injury suffered over a long period of time.

Reilly v Merseyside Regional Health Authority
(1994) 23 BMLR 26

A couple became trapped in a lift as the result of negligence and suffered insomnia and claustrophobia as a result. There was held to be no liability for nervous shock.

It was held that claims for nervous shock must involve an actual, recognised psychiatric condition capable of resulting from the shock of the incident, and recognised as having long-term effects. Claustrophobia was not accepted as a recognised psychiatric injury for the purposes of nervous shock.

CA **Vernon v Boseley** [1997] 1 All ER 577

A father had witnessed his children being drowned in a car that was being negligently driven by the children's nanny. He recovered damages for nervous shock that was held to be partly the result of pathological grief and bereavement, but partly also the consequence of the trauma of witnessing the events.

A secondary victim can claim if the psychiatric injury caused by the sudden traumatic event, even though it is based on profound grief is also linked to clinical depression.

CA **Calascione v Dixon** (1993) 19 BMLR 97

The defendant caused the death of a 20-year-old in a motorcycle accident. The mother of the young man then suffered nervous shock following the inquest and a private prosecution.

It was held that the nervous shock must be in fact caused by the single traumatic event. In other words, there must be a causal link between the event and the damage suffered. There was none here and so no liability.

2.5 Pure economic loss

Spartan Steel v Martin & Co. (Contractors) Ltd
[1973] 1 QB 27

The defendant cut an electric cable, causing loss of power to the claimant, who made steel alloys. A 'melt' in the claimant's furnace when the power cut occurred had to be destroyed or it would have set and wrecked the furnace. The claimant also lost profit on further 'melts' that it could have made during the power cut. The claimant successfully claimed for physical damage and lost profit from the 'melt' in the furnace, but was refused the further loss of profit.

The loss was foreseeable. However, the court held that it was not possible to recover for pure economic loss caused by a negligent act since policy dictated that the loss was better borne by the insurers than by the defendants alone.

Lord Denning explained:
'It seems to me better to consider the particular relationship in hand, and see whether or not, as a matter of policy, economic loss should be recoverable or not.'

Murphy v Brentwood District Council [1991] 2 All ER 908

A council approved plans for a concrete raft on which properties were built. The raft was inadequate and later moved causing cracks in the walls and gas pipes to break. The claimant lost £35,000 from the value of his house and sought damages.

The court held that, in the absence of any injury, loss was purely economic, and could not be recovered. Local authorities will not be liable for the cost of repairing dangerous defects unless injury occurs as well. The court also overruled *Anns*.

2.6 Negligent misstatement

2.6.1 The origins of liability

HL **Hedley Byrne v Heller & Partners Ltd**
[1964] AC 465

The claimant, an advertising company, was asked to produce a campaign for a small company. Because it had not previously dealt with that company it sought a credit reference from the company's bank, which gave a satisfactory reference without checking on the company's current financial standing. The claimant produced the campaign but then the company went into liquidation and so the claimant could not be paid for its work. The claimant sued the bank for its negligently made advice but failed because the bank had included a disclaimer of liability in its credit reference.

The House *in obiter* approved Lord Denning's dissenting judgment from *Candler v Crane Christmas & Co* and held that it is possible to recover for a purely financial loss caused by a negligently made statement if certain conditions are met.

> Lord Reid explained:
> 'A reasonable man, knowing that he was being
> trusted or that his skill and judgment were being
> relied on, would ... be held to have accepted some
> responsibility for his answer being given carefully,
> or to have accepted a relationship with the inquirer
> which requires him to exercise such care as the
> circumstances require.'
>
> ➤ *Candler v Crane Christmas & Co.* [1951] 2 KB 164

2.6.2 The criteria for imposing liability

PC **Mutual Life and Citizens Assurance Co. Ltd v Evatt**
[1971] AC 793

The claimant asked an insurance company agent to give advice
about the products of another company with which he
planned to invest. The advice was inaccurate and the claimant
lost money.

The court held that there was no duty owed in the
circumstances because the defendant had not held himself out
as being in the business of giving the type of advice asked for.

CA **Chaudhry v Prabhaker** [1988] 3 All ER 718

The claimant asked a friend, with some experience of cars, to
find her a good second-hand car. When it was later discovered
that the car had been in an accident and was not completely
roadworthy the claimant successfully sued her friend.

The court held that the relationship for the purpose of the advice operated in a similar way to principal and agent and so was sufficient to impose a duty of care on the person giving the advice.

This is a strange result as it is generally accepted that no duty is owed in a purely social relationship.

HL | Smith v Eric S Bush [1990] 2 WLR 790

A building society valuation identified that chimney breasts had been removed, but the valuer failed to check whether the bricks above were properly secured. They were not and after the purchase they collapsed and the purchaser sued successfully.

The court held that there was a duty of care because, even though the contract was the between building society and valuer, it was reasonably foreseeable that the purchaser would rely on it.

CA | Goodwill v British Pregnancy Advisory Service [1996] 2 All ER 161

The defendant failed properly to advise a patient of the possibility that his vasectomy could automatically reverse itself. The claimant had become pregnant after relying on the man informing her that he had had a vasectomy.

The court held that a doctor can not be fixed with liability to the future partners of patients who they have performed a vasectomy on. The class is potentially too wide and unforeseeable. The court rejected the link drawn with *White v Jones*.

2.6.3 The current state of the law

HL **Henderson v Merrett Syndicates** [1994] 3 All ER 506

Insurance underwriters lost huge sums because of negligent management of the syndicates of which they were members and needed to prove that the managing agents owed them a duty in tort as well as contractual duties.

The court held that there was a duty because of an assumption of responsibility by the defendants. The court added this requirement to the list for establishing liability from *Caparo v Dickman* (1990).

- the advice must be required for a purpose described at the time to the defendant at least in general terms;
- this purpose must be made known actually or by inference to the party giving the advice at the time it is given;
- if the advice will subsequently be communicated to the party relying on it, this fact must be known by the adviser;
- the adviser must be aware that the advice will be acted upon without benefit of any further independent advice;
- the person alleging to have relied on the advice must show actual reliance and consequent detriment suffered;
- the person giving the advice must have assumed responsibility.

Caparo v Dickman [1990] 2 AC 605

2.6.4 Cases inconsistent with the general principle

HL **White v Jones** [1995] 1 All ER 691

Solicitors failed to draw up a will before the testator's death and the intended beneficiaries consequently lost their inheritance.

The court held that a duty was owed to the beneficiaries even though the contractual relationship was with the testator, and since a will can be changed a beneficiary is not necessarily ensured the inheritance. Nevertheless, the House was prepared to identify both a special relationship in the circumstances and reliance.

2.7 Omissions

HL **Smith v Littlewoods Organisation Ltd** [1987] 1 All ER 710

The defendant bought a cinema to demolish and rebuild as a supermarket and then left it empty. Vandals broke in and set fire to it. The fire spread and caused damage to the claimants' properties.

The court held that there was no liability. The defendant could not be responsible for acts of strangers of which it had no knowledge.

Lord Goff in the House of Lords stated:
'In such a case it is not possible to invoke a general duty of
care; for it is well recognised that there is no general duty of
care to prevent third parties from causing such damage.'

Lord Goff also identified the situations in which a party could
be liable for an omission – where the defendant owes a duty
to act:

- because of a contractual or other undertaking;
- because of a special relationship with the claimant;
- because of damage that is done by a third party who is
  within his control;
- because he has control of things on his land or other
  dangerous things.

HL **Home Office v Dorset Yacht Co. Ltd** [1970] AC 1004

Seven Borstal boys on a training camp in Poole, five of whom
had escaped before, escaped when the warders, against their
instructions, were all asleep. The boys caused considerable
damage to yachts in the harbour. The claim for damages
against the Home Office was successful.

The Home Office was held liable for its employees' failure to
control the offenders in their charge because its employees had
failed in their duty to restrain the boys and protect the public
from them.

PC **Goldman v Hargrave** [1967] 1 AC 645

A 100-foot-high tree on the defendant's land was struck by lightning and ignited. The defendant cleared land around the tree, felled it and cut the burning tree into sections to burn out. When a high wind developed the fire from the tree spread to neighbouring property causing extensive damage. The defendant was liable.

The court acknowledged that the defendant had done nothing positive to cause the spread of fire or increase the risk of damage. Nevertheless, he failed to do something which he could have done with little extra cost or effort than he had already made, put the fire out. On this basis, he was negligent.

OCCUPIERS' LIABILITY

Occupiers' Liability Act 1957 (lawful visitors)
Glasgow Corporation v Taylor (1922)
The occupier must expect children to be less cautious than adults, has a higher standard of care, and must avoid 'allurements'
Phipps v Rochester Corporation (1955)
But can expect parents to be responsible for very young children
Roles v Nathan (1963)
The occupier can rely on the skill and knowledge of people entering to exercise a trade or calling to avoid risks associated with the work
Haseldine v Daw (1941)
The occupier is not liable for the work done by independent contractors if it was reasonable to hire them, a competent contractor is chosen and the work is checked if the nature of the work allows
Staples v West Dorset DC (1995)
The occupier may use warning signs to avoid liability but has no need when the danger is obvious to a reasonable man
White v Blakemore (1972)
Consent is only a defence where the visitor freely accepts the actual risk

---

Definition of 'occupier'
Wheat v Lacon (1966)
A person who is in actual control of the premises when the damage occurs

Occupiers' liability

Occupiers' Liability Act 1984 (trespassers)
BR Board v Herrington (1972)
Introduced the 'common duty of humanity' through common law
Tomlinson v Congleton BC (2003)
The Act can apply if the danger is due to the state of the premises, and is the sort of risk that the defendant should have guarded against and one that the trespasser in fact chose to run
Ratcliffe v McConnell (1999)
Volenti applies and liability is avoided if the claimant freely accepted the actual risk of harm

3.1 Liability to lawful visitors under the 1957 Act

3.1.1 Definition of 'occupier'

HL **Wheat v E Lacon & Co Ltd** [1966] AC 552

A pub manager was allowed to rent out rooms in his private quarters even though he was not the owner. An action arose because a paying guest fell on an unlit staircase, although as it was later identified, a stranger had removed the bulb so there was no liability on either the pub manager or the brewery.

The House of Lords held that an occupier was someone in 'actual control of the premises at the time when the damage was caused'. This meant that both the landlord and the manager could potentially be liable.

3.1.2 Liability to children

HL **Glasgow Corporation v Taylor** [1922] I AC 44

A seven-year-old boy was poisoned when he ate berries in an area of botanical gardens which was not fenced off in any way. The subsequent negligence claim was successful.

The court held that occupiers must anticipate that children are less cautious than adults and that the berries amounted to an 'allurement'. Occupiers must take greater care of children than they would of adults.

s2(3) Occupiers' Liability Act 1957: occupiers 'must be prepared for children to be less careful than adults ... the premises must be reasonably safe for a child of that age'.

QBD **Phipps v Rochester Corporation** [1955] 1 QB 450

A five-year-old boy was injured one evening when he fell in a nine-feet-deep trench dug by the defendants' workers, near which children often played. The claim for compensation failed.

The court held that the occupier (the local council) was not in breach of its duty of care as parents of young children have a duty to prevent them from coming into contact with danger.

Devlin J stated:
'Even if it be prudent, which I do not think it is, for a parent to allow two small children out in this way on an October evening, the parents might at least have satisfied themselves that the place to which they allowed these little children to go held no dangers for them ... defendants are entitled to assumed that parents would behave in this naturally prudent way, and are not obliged to take it on themselves, in effect, to discharge parental duties.'

HL **Jolley v London Borough of Sutton** [2000] 3 All ER 409

Two 14-year-old boys were injured on an abandoned boat on the Council's land. Children regularly played in the boat and it was an obvious danger but the Council had failed to remove it for two years. The boys had been injured while jacking up the boat and trying to repair it. The Court of Appeal had held that there was no liability since the circumstances in which the injuries had occurred was unforeseeable. The House of Lords reversed this decision.

The House of Lords held that, as long as the boat created a foreseeable risk of injury, then the precise circumstances in which the injury occurred was not material in imposing liability.

Hughes v Lord Advocate [1963] AC 387

3.1.3 Liability to persons entering under a trade or calling

CA **Roles v Nathan** [1963] 1 WLR 1117

Two chimney sweeps, who were cleaning flues in a factory, died after inhaling fumes. There was no liability because they had been warned by the occupier of the danger of working in the chimney while the furnace was lit but had ignored the advice.

The occupier may assume that professional visitors will guard against risks that are within their professional knowledge.

3.1.4 Liability for the torts of independent contractors

Haseldine v Daw & Sons Ltd [1941] 2 KB 343

The claimant was killed following the negligent repair of a lift on the occupier's premises. The occupier had hired reputable contractors for a highly technical procedure and successfully defended the claim on this basis.

There was no liability because the technical nature of the repairs meant that the occupier was not equipped to check the work and could rely on the skill and expertise of the contractor.

s 2(4)(b) Occupiers' Liability Act 1957

The section identifies that an occupier can avoid liability if it is reasonable for him to entrust the work to an independent contractor, and that he has taken reasonable steps to ensure that a competent contractor has been hired and that the work has been carried out properly.

CA **Woodward v Hastings Corporation** [1945] KB 174

A child was injured on school steps that had been left in an icy state when they had been cleared of snow by contractors. The claim for damages against the occupier succeeded.

Liability stayed with the occupier since checking on the standard of the work was straightforward because of the type of work.

In commenting on the occupier's responsibility Lord Denning identified that: 'there is no esoteric quality in the nature of the work which the cleaning of a snow covered step demands.'

CA **Gwillam v West Hertfordshire NHS Trust**
[2002] 3 WLR 1425

The hospital trust held a fund raising fair on its premises and hired a 'splat wall' from a firm, Club Entertainments, that was also responsible for operating it. (A 'splat wall' is a wall to which a person wearing a Velcro suit will stick after bouncing from a trampoline.) The wall was poorly assembled by the firm and the claimant fell, injuring herself. Club Entertainments was bound under the contract with the trust to have public liability insurance but this had expired four days before the fair so when the claimant sued the trust for damages she was unsuccessful.

Lord Woolf CJ and Lord Justice Waller held that, while ensuring that contractors were ensured was part of the duty of hiring competent contractors, the duty had not been breached here and the contractors held the duty of ensuring that the claimant was safe to use the 'splat wall'.

Bottomley v Todmorden Cricket Club [2003] EWCA Civ 1575

3.1.5 Avoiding liability

CA **Staples v West Dorset DC** (1995) 93 LGR 536

The claimant slipped on wet algae on a high wall at Lyme Regis, injuring himself. His claim against the council was unsuccessful.

The court held that the danger should have been obvious and there was therefore no additional duty to warn of the danger.

CA **White v Blakemore** [1972] 3 All ER 158

The claimant, who was a competitor in a 'jalopy race', was killed while standing in front of a rope barrier to a spectators' enclosure. A car crashed into the barrier and caused it to catapult him into the air. A prominently displayed notice excluded liability. A claim failed on his behalf.

The court held that he was an implied licensee, but the defence of *volenti non fit injuria* under s 2(5) of the 1957 Act was inapplicable because the claimant could not have consented to inadequate safety arrangements and was unaware of the full risk. However, the exclusion clause was effective.

3.2 Liability to trespassers under the 1984 Act

3.2.1 Common law and the duty of common humanity

HL **British Railways Board v Herrington** [1972] AC 877

A six-year-old was badly burned when straying onto an electrified railway line, through vandalised fencing. It was well known that the fences were often broken and that small children played near the line and the railway board regularly repaired it.

The House, using the Practice Statement, overruled the previous law in *Addie v Dumbreck* [1929] and established the 'common duty of humanity'. This was a limited duty owed to child trespassers when the occupier knew of the danger, and of the likelihood of the trespass, and had the skill, knowledge and resources to avoid an accident.

This duty would obviously operate in fairly limited circumstances and was not without criticism or difficulties. Because of some of the impracticalities of the rule, the 1984 Act was passed.

➡

Robert Addie & Sons (Collieries) Ltd v Dumbreck [1929] All ER 1

Child trespassers were injured on industrial premises but denied a remedy by the rule that occupiers owed no duty of care to trespassers other than not to deliberately cause them harm.

3.2.2 When the Act applies

HL **Tomlinson v Congleton BC** [2003] 1 AC 46

A local authority owned a park in which there was a lake. It posted warning signs prohibiting swimming and diving because the water was dangerous, but the council knew that the signs were generally ignored. The council decided to make the lake inaccessible to the public but delayed start on this work because of lack of funds. The claimant, who was aged 18, dived into the lake, struck his head and suffered a severe spinal injury and was paralysed as a result. His claim under the 1984 Act was rejected by the trial judge but succeeded in the Court of Appeal. The House of Lords then upheld the appeal by the Council.

The Court of Appeal had held that all three aspects of s 1(3) were satisfied as it felt that the gravity of the risk of injury, the frequency with which people were exposed to the risk, and the fact that the lake acted as an allurement all meant that the scheme to make the lake inaccessible should have been completed with greater urgency, although it did acknowledge the contributory negligence of the claimant. The House of Lords, in accepting the council's appeal based its decision on three reasons: that the danger was not due to the state of the premises, that it was not the sort of risk that the defendant should have to guard against but one that the trespasser in fact chose to run, and that the council would not have breached its duty even in the case of a lawful visitor since the practicality and financial cost of avoiding the danger was beyond what should be expected of a reasonable occupier.

Lord Hoffmann stated that:
'A duty to protect [against] self-inflicted harm exists only in cases where there is … some lack of capacity, such as the inability of children to recognise danger'

3.2.3 Avoiding the duty

HL **Westwood v The Post Office** [1974] AC 1

The claimant was injured when he took an unauthorised break at work and fell through a defective trapdoor. A sign 'Only the authorised attendant is permitted to enter' on the door of a motor room was held sufficient warning for an intelligent adult.

The court held that there was a valid warning under s 1(5) and so there could be no liability.

There is still a question as to whether such warnings would succeed in the case of children who may be unable to read or may not fully understand the warning.

CA **Ratcliffe v McConnell** [1999] 1 WLR 670

A warning notice at the shallow end of a swimming pool read: 'Deep end shallow dive'. The pool was always kept locked after hours and the claimant knew that entry was prohibited at this time. He was a trespasser and so when he was injured while diving into the shallow end his claim failed.

The court held that the claimant was fully aware of the risk and that by s 1(6) the defence of *volenti non fit injuria* thus applied. The claimant had freely accepted the risk of harm.

CHAPTER 4

NUISANCE

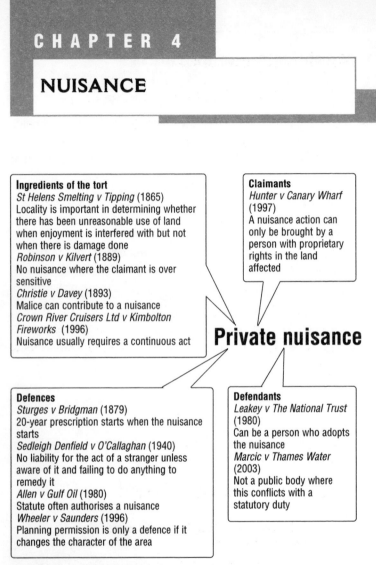

Ingredients of the tort
St Helens Smelting v Tipping (1865)
Locality is important in determining whether there has been unreasonable use of land when enjoyment is interfered with but not when there is damage done
Robinson v Kilvert (1889)
No nuisance where the claimant is over sensitive
Christie v Davey (1893)
Malice can contribute to a nuisance
Crown River Cruisers Ltd v Kimbolton Fireworks (1996)
Nuisance usually requires a continuous act

Claimants
Hunter v Canary Wharf (1997)
A nuisance action can only be brought by a person with proprietary rights in the land affected

Private nuisance

Defences
Sturges v Bridgman (1879)
20-year prescription starts when the nuisance starts
Sedleigh Denfield v O'Callaghan (1940)
No liability for the act of a stranger unless aware of it and failing to do anything to remedy it
Allen v Gulf Oil (1980)
Statute often authorises a nuisance
Wheeler v Saunders (1996)
Planning permission is only a defence if it changes the character of the area

Defendants
Leakey v The National Trust (1980)
Can be a person who adopts the nuisance
Marcic v Thames Water (2003)
Not a public body where this conflicts with a statutory duty

Public nuisance

Attorney-General v PYA Quarries Ltd (1957)
Public nuisance is one which affects the reasonable comfort and convenience of a class of Her Majesty's subjects
Castle v St Augustine Links (1922)
But the claimant must suffer special damage

4.1 Private nuisance

4.1.1 Potential claimants in nuisance

HL **Hunter and another v Canary Wharf** [1997] 2 All ER 426

Families of tenants made unsuccessful claims in private nuisance for dust and interference with television reception caused by the erection of a very large building near to their homes.

The court held that there was an interference with recreational facilities only, not with the health or physical wellbeing of the claimants. The House also held that the claimants could not in any case bring an action as they had no proprietary interest in the land.

Lord Goff explained:
'an action in nuisance will only lie at the suit of a person who has a right to the land affected'.

4.1.2 The ingredients of the tort

HL **St Helens Smelting Co. v Tipping**
(1865) 11 HL Cas 642

The claimant owned property near to the defendant's copper smelting works and claimed in nuisance for damage to hedges and trees caused by the toxic smuts and interference with his quiet enjoyment of his land. He succeeded.

The court held that the nuisance was actionable because, even though it involved an industrial area, damage had been caused.

Lord Westbury LC stated:
'With regard to ... personal inconvenience and interference with one's enjoyment ... whether that may ... be ... a nuisance, must undoubtedly depend ... on ... the place where the thing complained of actually occurs ... when an occupation is carried on ... and the result ... is a material injury to property, then there unquestionably arises a very different consideration.'

QBD **Laws v Florinplace Ltd** [1981] 1 All ER 659

Ten residents in a suburban area, enjoying what was described as an 'attractive village atmosphere', successfully sought an injunction against a sex shop and video club that had opened in their area.

The court held that even if the defendant changed the name of the business and its name and its displays, it was still arguable that the repugnance caused to the residents by their awareness of the business could be an interference amounting to a nuisance.

CA | **Robinson v Kilvert** (1889) 41 ChD 88

The claimant stored paper in premises where the defendant manufactured cardboard boxes in the basement. The heat necessary for the manufacture damaged the brown paper and the claimant unsuccessfully sought damages in nuisance.

The court held that the heating was not a nuisance since it was not of a sort that would cause damage in the case of the ordinary uses of the premises. Damage was only caused because the brown paper was very susceptible to variations in temperature.

Ch Div | **Christie v Davey** [1893] 1 Ch 316

The claimant gave music lessons and the defendant, his next-door neighbour, became annoyed by the constant noise from the music lessons next door. The defendant reacted by banging on the walls, beating trays and shouting.

The court held that the noises were made maliciously and deliberately to annoy the claimant. They were an unreasonable use of land and the claimant was granted an injunction.

Hollywood Silver Fox Farm Ltd v Emmet [1936] 2 KB 468

QBD Halsey v Esso Petroleum Co. Ltd [1961] 2 All ER 145

The claimant won a claim for nuisance from the noise from the defendant's depot, the nauseating smell and also in relation to the damage which acid smuts caused to her washing and to her car.

The court held that they were all private nuisance except for the damage to the car which was a public nuisance. The defendant's use of land was unreasonable.

Veale J stated:
'the law must strike a fair and reasonable balance between the rights of the plaintiff on the one hand to the undisturbed enjoyment of his property, and the right of the defendant on the other hand to use his own property for his own lawful enjoyment'.

QBD Crown River Cruisers Ltd v Kimbolton Fireworks Ltd [1996] 2 Lloyd's Rep 533

A barge was set alight by flammable debris resulting from a firework display which lasted only 20 minutes. The owners claimed successfully in negligence and it was also accepted that the action in private nuisance was also possible.

The court held that an action for nuisance was possible because the barge owners had a licence to occupy the site.

The very limited duration of the display seems to run contrary to the principle of continuity required for nuisance, e.g. *Bolton v Stone* (1951).

CA Holbeck Hall Hotel Ltd v Scarborough BC
[2000] 2 All ER 705

The claimant's hotel stood near to a cliff by the sea. The defendant, the local council, owned the land between the hotel and the cliff top. After a long period of steady erosion a major landslip undermined the foundations of the hotel so that it had to be demolished. On appeal, the council was held not to be liable in nuisance.

The Court of Appeal held that, since the council was unaware of the danger of the landslip, which could not merely be presumed from the previous erosion, it neither adopted nor created the nuisance.

Stuart-Smith LJ explained that:
'It is the existence of the defect coupled with the danger that constitutes the nuisance; it is knowledge ... of the nuisance that involves liability for continuing it when it could have been abated.'

4.1.3 Potential defendants in nuisance

Leakey v The National Trust [1980] QB 485

Following heavy rain, a large natural mound of land on a hillside, known as the Burrow Mump, slipped and damaged the claimant's cottage. The defendant was held liable in nuisance.

The court found the defendant liable because it was aware of the possibility of the landslide happening and did nothing to prevent it.

The case shows what a close link there is between nuisance and negligence. The type of duty depends on the facts of the case.

Tetley and others v Chitty and others [1986] 1 All ER 663

The defendant council rented land to another party on which to run go-kart racing. Local residents succeeded in gaining an injunction.

The court held the council liable because it was already aware of the excessive noise that the activity would cause and had accepted responsibility for the nuisance by granting the lease.

HL **Marcic v Thames Water plc**
[2003] UKHL 66; [2003] 3 WLR 1603

Because of the substantial rise in the number of houses in an area the sewers, which had not been modified, became inadequate to cope with the amount of sewage, even though the defendant maintained them properly. The sewers flooded periodically and the claimant, rather than using statutory enforcement measures, installed a flood defence and claimed for damages in nuisance and for interference in family life in breach of Art 8 of the European Convention on Human Rights. Both claims failed.

The House held that there was no actionable nuisance since the common law would be unable to impose obligations on a water authority which were inconsistent with a statutory scheme and in this instance the right of complaint was to the Director-General of Water Services. There was no breach of Human Rights legislation since Art 8 of the European Convention does not guarantee absolute protection of residential properties but must balance out the rights of individuals and the rights of the public generally.

4.1.4 Defences

CA **Sturges v Bridgman** (1879) 11 ChD 852

Eight years after he moved in, a doctor built a consulting room at the bottom of his garden. Vibrations from the defendant's machinery in the neighbouring property disturbed the claimant and prevented him from listening to his patients' chests etc. His claim succeeded

The court held that the defence could not apply because the twenty year period for prescription would only begin when the nuisance commenced, here when the consulting room was built.

CA **Miller v Jackson** [1977] QB 966

A new housing estate was built by a cricket club that had been used for 70 years. Balls constantly came into the claimant's garden during matches and he succeeded in claims in both nuisance and negligence, but was denied the injunction that he sought.

The court held that while there was a plain interference with the claimant's enjoyment of his land it recognised that the remedy could not be granted because it would interfere with a public utility of importance to the community.

Lord Denning dissented on the decision because, as he said, playing cricket 'is a most reasonable use of land'. On refusing to grant the injunction, he said 'I recognise that the cricket club are under a duty to use all reasonable care ... but I do not think the cricket club can be expected to give up the game of cricket altogether'.

Sedleigh Denfield v O'Callaghan [1940] AC 880

A workman had placed grating for trapping leaves too close to a culvert pipe on the defendant's land. The defendant knew about it. After a severe storm the pipe became blocked, his neighbours land was flooded. His neighbour succeeded in his nuisance claim.

On appeal, the court held that the defendant was liable because he was aware of the nuisance but failed to do anything to remedy it and so had adopted the nuisance. The defence of act of a stranger was not applicable in the circumstances.

Lord Wright said:
'The responsibility which attaches to the occupier because he has possession and control of the property cannot logically be limited to the mere creation of the nuisance. It should extend to ... if, with knowledge, he leaves the nuisance on his land.'

HL ## Allen v Gulf Oil Refining Ltd [1980] QB 156

The claimants sued for nuisance caused by a refinery. An Act authorised the defendants to purchase land for the construction of a refinery but made no mention of its use. The claim failed.

On appeal, the court held that the statutory authorisation for construction of a refinery necessarily implied its use as a refinery. The defence of statutory authority succeeded.

CA **Wheeler v J J Saunders Ltd [1996] Ch 19**

The defendant, a pig farmer, was granted planning permission to expand by building two more pig houses each containing 400 pigs. One pig house was only 11 metres from the cottage of a neighbour who then successfully claimed in nuisance.

The defendant's appeal on the defence of planning permission failed because the defence was said to operate only in respect of those nuisances that Parliament had authorised.

Peter Gibson LJ explained that planning permission can only be a defence where as the result of the permitted activity 'there will be a change in the character of the neighbourhood.'

➤

Gillingham Borough Council v Medway (Chatham) Dock Co. [1993] QB 343

CA ## 4.1.5 Remedies

Kennaway v Thompson [1981] 3 WLR 311

The claimant built a house near to a lake where speed boat racing had taken place for many years. He succeeded in his claim for nuisance created by the excessive noise.

At first instance the claimant was awarded £1,600 in damages. On appeal he was granted an injunction restraining the use of the lake for speed boat races to certain days with certain noise limits.

4.2 Public nuisance

CA **Attorney-General v PYA Quarries Ltd** [1957] 2 QB 169

Houses neighbouring a quarry suffered from dust and vibrations. The Attorney-General successfully sought injunctions on behalf of the County Council and the District Council.

The court rejected the defendant's argument that the nuisance was not sufficiently widespread to amount to a public nuisance.

Romer LJ stated:
'any nuisance is "public" which materially affects the reasonable comfort and convenience of life of a class of Her Majesty's subjects.'

QBD **Castle v St Augustine Links** (1922) 38 TLR 615

A taxi driver was hit in the eye by a sliced golf ball. The golf links straddled the highway so the risk of harm was great and it was shown that golf balls regularly came off the course and onto the road. The claim in public nuisance succeeded.

The court accepted that the regularity of the occurrence was a significant interference with the public's use of the highway and the claimant had suffered special damage so the nuisance was proved.

CHAPTER 5

STRICT LIABILITY

Rylands v Fletcher (1868)
Giles v Walker (1890)
No liability for things naturally present on the land
Rickards v Lothian (1913)
A domestic water supply is not a non-natural use of land
Mason v Levy Auto Parts (1967)
But potentially dangerous things stored in extremely large quantities are
Read v Lyons (1947)
The thing must escape from land over which the defendant has control to land
over which he has no control
Hale v Jennings (1948)
It is arguable whether the tort extends to personal injuries
Cambridge Water v Eastern Counties Leather (1994)
There must be foreseeable damage as the result of the escape
Perry v Kendricks Transport (1956)
Act of a stranger is a common defence
Green v Chelsea Waterworks (1894)
As is statutory authority

Strict liability

Animals Act 1971
Tutin v Mary Chipperfield Promotions (1980)
Strict liability for dangerous species – those not commonly domesticated in the
UK because damage caused could be severe
Curtis v Betts (1990)
All three subsections in s 2 must be proved for a successful claim where the
species is non-dangerous
Mirvahedy v Henley (2003)
Even though the behaviour of the animal may be unusual if it is reasonable to
assume such behaviour will occur in the circumstances then the keeper is liable
Dhesi v Chief Constable of the West Midlands Police (2000)
Defences include s 5(1) where the injury was entirely the claimant's own fault and
s 5(2) where the claimant freely accepted the risk of harm

5.1 *Rylands v Fletcher*

5.1.1 Definition, purpose and character of the rule

CE and HL | **Rylands v Fletcher**
(1868) LR I Exch 265; LR 3 HL 330

The defendant, a mill owner, hired contractors to create a reservoir on his land to supply water to the mill. The contractors carelessly failed to block off disused mineshafts which, unknown to the contractors, were connected to other mine works on adjoining land. When the reservoir was filled it flooded these neighbouring mines, causing damage.

While the facts did not fit easily into the law of nuisance as the case did not involve continuity, it was held that there could be liability for the accumulation of things that were not naturally present on the land which escaped and caused damage. Lord Cairns in the House of Lords added the requirement that the accumulation must amount to a 'non-natural' use of land for there to be liability.

Blackburn J. in the Court of Exchequer explained the rule in the following way:
'We think that the true rule of law is, that the person who, for purposes of his own, brings on his land and keeps there anything likely to do mischief if it escapes, must keep it in at his peril, and, if he does not do so, he is prima facie answerable for all the damage which is the natural consequence of its escape.'

It is generally agreed that the judges were creating an entirely new legal principle. A possible reason is that judges then were from the landed elite and resented the new wealth of the industrialists so wished to create a strict liability rule to prevent industrial pollution.

5.1.2 The ingredients of the rule

QBD **Giles v Walker** (1890) 24 QBD 656

A claim for damage resulting from the defendant allowing weeds growing on his land to accumulate and spread to his neighbour's land was unsuccessful.

There was held to be no liability for things not naturally present on the land. The rule requires artificial accumulation.

CA **Miles v Forest Rock Granite Co. (Leicestershire) Ltd** (1918) 34 TLR 500 CA

The claimant brought a successful claim for injury suffered when rocks flew onto the highway from the defendant's land where blasting was being carried out.

Even though it was the explosives that had been brought onto land rather than the rock itself which was naturally present, it was the blasting that had actually caused the rock to escape. It was held that in such circumstances it need not be the actual thing brought onto land that escapes.

KB Musgrove v Pandelis [1919] 2 KB 43

A car was kept in a garage with a full tank of petrol. When the petrol caught fire and the fire spread to the next door neighbour's house, although the fire was unlikely it was accepted that it would certainly cause mischief if it escaped.

Because of the small number of cars in existence at the time, the practice was held to be a non-natural use of land.

This demonstrates the unpredictability of the rule since the same practice would not be considered non-natural use of land today, with the modern extent of car ownership.

Rickards v Lothian [1913] AC 263

An unknown person turned on water taps and blocked plugholes on the defendant's premises so that damage was caused in the flat below. The defendant was held not liable.

There was held to be no liability not just because the defendant could successfully use the defence of act of a stranger but more importantly because a domestic water supply was not a non-natural use of land.

As Lord Moulton explained:
'It is not every use … that brings into play the principle … It

must be some special use bringing with it increased danger to others and must not be the ordinary use of the land or such a use as is proper for the benefit of the community.'

Mason v Levy Auto Parts of England [1967] 2 QB 530

The defendant stored large quantities of scrap tyres on his land. These were then ignited and the fire spread to the claimant's premises, causing great damage, and the claim under the rule was successful.

The judge identified that storage of such large quantities of combustible material; the casual way in which they were stored and the character of the neighbourhood were all factors in determining that there was a non-natural use of the land.

The case illustrates that it is the context in which the thing is accumulated as much as the thing itself that can determine that there is a non-natural use of land and possible liability.

HL **Read v Lyons** [1947] AC 156

A factory inspector was inspecting a munitions factory and was injured, along with a number of employees, one man dying, when some of the shells exploded. Her claim for damages failed.

The House of Lords held that the rule did not apply because there was 'no escape at all of the relevant kind'.

Viscount Simon explained that an escape in *Rylands v Fletcher* (1868) means 'an escape from a place where the defendant has occupation or control over land to a place which is outside his occupation or control'.

QBD British Celanese v A H Hunt (Capacitors) Ltd
[1969] 1 WLR 959

The defendant stored strips of metal foil on its land, for use in manufacturing electrical components. Some strips of foil blew off the defendants' land and onto an electricity substation, causing power failures to the claimant's factory. A claim was brought under negligence, private nuisance, public nuisance and under *Rylands v Fletcher* (1868) and the claim under the latter was dismissed.

The court held that the use of land was natural. This was partly because there were no unusual risks associated with the storage of the foil and partly because of the benefit derived by the public from the manufacture so the rule could not apply.

Lawton J identified also that escape means:
'from a set of circumstances over which the defendant had control to a set of circumstances where he does not.'

It has been suggested that this interpretation of 'non-natural' is very similar to the idea of unreasonable risk in negligence, making the tort indistinguishable from negligence.

5.1.3 The parties to an action

CA **Hale v Jennings Bros** [1948] 1 All ER 579

A stallholder on a fairground was injured when a car from a 'chair-o-plane' ride became detached from the main assembly while it was in motion and crashed to the ground. The owner of the ride was liable even though both parties occupied the same ground.

The court held that there was liability because risk of injury was foreseeable if the car came loose and because there was an escape from the defendant's control.

This clearly conflicts with the meaning of escape given in *Read v Lyons*, and extends the range of potential claimants.

➡️

Hunter v Canary Wharf [1997] AC 655: see p59

This is a major case in private nuisance that suggests that the rule may not extend to claims for personal injury.

5.1.4 Recoverable loss and remoteness of damage

HL **Cambridge Water Co. v Eastern Counties Leather plc** [1994] 2 WLR 53

The defendant owned a tannery and used a solvent to degrease the animal skins. Sometimes this solvent spilled onto the concrete floor and over a period of time it seeped into the ground and eventually filtered through into a borehole more than a mile away owned by the claimant Water Company and from which water for domestic consumption and use was extracted. The solvent contaminated the water and the claim for damages was unsuccessful.

 The House of Lords held that storage of chemicals could always be regarded as a non-natural use of land but that, since the contamination could not be foreseen by a reasonable person there could be no liability.

Adding the requirement of foreseeability to the essential elements of a claim under the tort Lord Goff identified that 'foreseeability of damage of the relevant type should be regarded as a prerequisite of liability ... under the rule.'

The addition of foresight of harm is a fault-based concept making the tort indistinguishable from negligence, casting doubt on whether the tort is in fact strict liability and making a successful claim almost impossible to bring.

HL **Transco plc v Stockport MBC**
[2003] UKHL 61; [2003] 3 WLR 1467

The defendant council built a block of multi-storey flats in which, without any negligence, the water pipes supplying the flats burst and water then escaped eventually causing an embankment to collapse, exposing the claimant's gas main and posing an immediate and serious risk. The claimant took immediate remedial action and unsuccessfully sought to recover the cost.

The House held that the claim could not succeed because it did not involve a non-natural use of land. The judges reviewed the law and identified *in obiter* that *Rylands v Fletcher* (1868) is still good law and approved the views expressed in *Cambridge Water* (1994) that it is a specific type of private nuisance, requiring foreseeable harm and that it is thus unavailable in claims for personal injury.

Lord Bingham did cast doubt on the concept of non-natural use of land:
'I think it is clear that ordinary user is a preferable test to natural user, making it clear that the rule … is engaged only where the defendant's use is shown to be extraordinary and unusual … I also doubt whether a test of reasonable user is helpful, since a user may well be quite out of the ordinary but not unreasonable …'

5.1.5 Possible defences

CA **Peters v Prince of Wales Theatre (Birmingham) Ltd** [1943] KB 73

The claimant rented a kiosk in a theatre. His stock was damaged by water from the defendant's sprinkler system. His claim failed.

It was held that the water supply was a natural use of land in context and for the benefit of both parties so that the claimant consented to the risk, and there was no liability for the escape.

CA | Perry v Kendricks Transport Ltd [1956] 1 WLR 85

The defendant parked its bus on its parking space after draining the petrol tank. When an unknown person removed the petrol cap a child was then injured when another child threw in a lit match, igniting the fumes in the tank. The claim for personal injury failed.

The court accepted that the rule could apply and also that an action for personal injury was possible under the rule. However, the damage was caused by an act of a stranger. It considered that the claimant had the burden of proof to show that such an eventuality was foreseeable. There was a valid defence and no liability.

CA | Green v Chelsea Waterworks Co. (1894) 70 LT 547

The defendants were obliged by statute to provide a water supply. The water supply was inevitably pressurised and when a burst pipe occurred water escaped, causing damage to the claimant whose action for damages was unsuccessful.

The court held that from time to time burst pipes were an inevitable consequence of the statutory duty, which provided an obvious defence, and there could be no liability without proof of negligence.

Lindley LJ commented that the rule:
'is not to be extended beyond the legitimate principle on

which the House of Lords decided it. If it were extended as far as strict logic might require, it would be a very oppressive decision'.

5.2 Liability for animals

5.2.1 Common law torts

CA **Draper v Hodder** [1972] 2 QB 556

A child was savaged by a pack of Jack Russell Terriers that were rushing from their owner's house next door. They had never acted this way before, so there could be no liability under the Animals Act 1971. The claimant was successful under negligence.

The court held that it was known that the breed of dog characteristically attacks in packs so there was foreseeable risk of harm and negligence.

5.2.2 The Animals Act 1971: dangerous species

QBD **Tutin v Mary Chipperfield Promotions Ltd** (1980) 130 NLJ 807

The claimant was injured when she was thrown off a camel during a camel race at the Horse of the Year Show. She succeeded in her negligence claim but failed under the Animals Act 1971.

The court accepted that the camel was a member of a dangerous species within the definition in s 6(2) of the Act,

even though this conflicted with a previous decision in
McQuaker v Goddard [1940] 1 KB 687 which held that a
camel is not a dangerous species because there is nowhere in
the world where a camel is wild. The court applied that part of
s 6(2) 'that any damage that they may cause is likely to be
severe'. However, the action would fail because the claimant
by agreeing to take part in the race had voluntarily accepted
the risk of harm within the meaning of s 5(2) of the Act.

For definition of dangerous see s 6(2) Animals Act 1971

5.2.3 The Animals Act 1971: non-dangerous species

CA **Cummings v Grainger** [1977] 1 All ER 104

An owner of a scrap yard allowed an untrained Alsatian to
roam free at night. The dog savaged a woman who entered
with her boyfriend who worked there. The woman's claim for
damages under the 1971 Act was unsuccessful.

The claim failed because, under s 5(2), the woman had
voluntarily accepted the risk of harm, she knew the dog was
dangerous and was frightened of it, and also because, at that
time, under s 5(3), it was held to be reasonable to keep a
guard dog in a scrap yard in the East End of London.

Lord Denning identified that the case was one where:
'the keeper of the dog is strictly liable unless he can bring
himself within one of the exceptions ... because the three

requirements ... are satisfied ... Section 2(2)(a): ... if it did bite anyone the damage was "likely to be severe". Section 2(2)(b): this animal was a guard dog ... on the defendant's own evidence it used to bark and run around in circles ... characteristics ... not normally found in Alsatian dogs except ... where they are used as guard dogs. Section 2(2)(c): those characteristics were known to the defendant.'

The Guard Dogs Act 1995 – which would probably have produced a different result since it is now a criminal offence for guard dogs to roam premises without a handler.

CA **Curtis v Betts** [1990] 1 All ER 769

The claimant was an 11-year-old boy who succeeded in his action for personal injury. The boy was bitten on the face by a 70kg bull mastiff dog called Max whom he knew well and whom he had called as he was passing the car that Max was being put into. Evidence showed that a characteristic of bull mastiffs was defence of territory and also that Max regarded the car as his own territory.

The court held that no defences under s 5 or contributory negligence applied and, although Max was considered to be a docile animal, that the damage he was likely to cause if unrestrained was likely to be severe. The court also held that s 2(2)(b) should be interpreted to mean that there should be a causal link between the characteristics of the animal and the type of damage suffered.

Slade LJ said:

'Lord Denning MR in *Cummings v Grainger* described s 2(2)
as "very cumbrously worded" and giving rise to "several
difficulties". I agree. Particularly in view of the somewhat
tortuous wording of the subsection, I think it desirable to
consider each of the three requirements separately and
in turn'.

HL **Mirvahedy v Henley**
   [2003] UKHL 16; [2003] 2 AC 491

The defendant kept horses in a field. Something
frightened the horses and they escaped eventually
onto a major road. There was then a collision
between one of the horses and the claimant's car,
in which the claimant suffered personal injury.
The defendant's appeal in the House of Lords was
unsuccessful. The key issue was the characteristics
of the animals.

The House of Lords, by a majority of three to two,
held that s 2(2)(b) applied. Even though the
behaviour of the horses was unusual for the species
for the most part, it was nevertheless normal for
the species in the particular circumstances.

Lord Walker gave the reason for imposing liability:
'It is common knowledge (and was known to the
appellants in this case) that horses, if exposed to a
very frightening stimulus, will panic and stampede,
knocking down obstacles in their path ... and may
continue their flight for considerable distance.
Horses loose in that state ... are an obvious danger
on a road carrying fast moving traffic. The
appellants knew these facts; they could decide

whether to run the risks involved in keeping horses … Although I feel sympathy for the appellants, who were held not to have been negligent in the fencing of the field, I see nothing unjust or unreasonable in the appellants having to bear the loss…'.

 The problem with this interpretation of s 2 is that it means that almost any circumstances in which a domestic animal causes harm could be classed as characteristics only exhibited at particular times. This would have the effect of extending liability to almost unlimited proportions.

5.2.4 The Animals Act 1971: defences

CA **Dhesi v Chief Constable of the West Midlands Police,** *The Times*, 9 May, 2000

Police had tracked the claimant, who was armed with a hockey stick, after a violent confrontation. When the claimant hid in bushes he was repeatedly warned that the dog would be set free unless he came out. The claimant was bitten when trying to escape from the dog, but was unsuccessful in his claim for personal injury.

The court held that the claimant had caused his own injury and had accepted the risk of being injured through his actions. There was a valid defence under both s 5(1) and s 5(2) and no liability.

CHAPTER 6

TRESPASS TO LAND

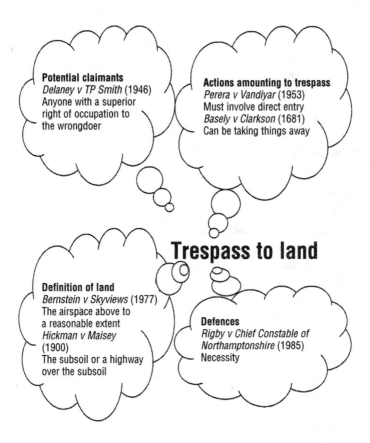

Potential claimants
Delaney v TP Smith (1946)
Anyone with a superior
right of occupation to
the wrongdoer

Actions amounting to trespass
Perera v Vandiyar (1953)
Must involve direct entry
Basely v Clarkson (1681)
Can be taking things away

Trespass to land

Definition of land
Bernstein v Skyviews (1977)
The airspace above to
a reasonable extent
Hickman v Maisey
(1900)
The subsoil or a highway
over the subsoil

Defences
*Rigby v Chief Constable of
Northamptonshire* (1985)
Necessity

6.1 Potential claimants

 Delaney v T P Smith & Co. [1946] KB 393

By an oral agreement, the claimant was to acquire a tenancy of the defendant's property. Before the lease was executed the claimant secretly entered the premises. The defendant then ejected the claimant who unsuccessfully sued for trespass.

The court held that, since the agreement had not been reduced to writing, the defendant still had superior rights of occupation.

Tucker LJ said:
'no doubt … a plaintiff need only in the first instance allege possession. This is sufficient to support his action against a wrongdoer, but … not … against the lawful owner'.

6.2 Actions amounting to a trespass

CA **Perera v Vandiyar** [1953] 1 WLR 672

The claimant was a tenant in the defendant's property. His gas and electricity meters were situated in the defendant's cellar. When the defendant switched off both supplies and the claimant was left for two days without heat or light he claimed damages unsuccessfully.

The court held on appeal that, while there was a clear interference with the claimant's premises, there was no direct entry which would be an absolute requirement for trespass.

CP **Basely v Clarkson** (1681) 3 Lev 37

The defendant cut and carried away some grass from his neighbour's strip of land. The claimant alleged trespass.

The court held that this was trespass even though it was carried out by mistake. However, the defendant had offered 2 shillings (10p) in full satisfaction which was accepted as discharging the issue.

6.3 The definition of 'land' in trespass

QBD **Lord Bernstein of Leigh v Skyviews & General Ltd**
[1977] QB 479

A company specialising in aerial photographs flew over the claimant's land, took photographs, and then tried to sell them to him. It was held not to be a trespass.

It was held that the claimant did have rights over the airspace above his property but that these should only extend to a height 'reasonably necessary for the enjoyment of the land'.

The Civil Aviation Act 1982 confirms this. Aircraft are generally immune from actions for trespass except where things fall from an aircraft or where aircraft make unauthorised landings.

QBD **Kelsen v Imperial Tobacco Co. Ltd** [1956] 2 QB 334

The defendant's advertising hoarding overhung the neighbouring land by 8 inches. An injunction to remove the sign succeeded.

The court held that there was a trespass because the sign invaded the claimant's airspace.

CA **Harrison v Duke of Rutland** [1893] 1 QB 142

The Duke commonly held grouse shoots on his land. Protesters gathered on the highway next to his land and tried to scare off the grouse. The Duke's action for trespass succeeded.

The court held that since the highway ran over the Duke's land it gave him rights over it and the defendants were liable because they used the highway improperly.

CA **Hickman v Maisey** [1900] 1 QB 752

The defendant used the highway to spy on the claimant's race horses in training and find out information on their performance before they entered races. The claimant's action succeeded.

The court held that there was a trespass since the defendant was using the adjoining highway for improper purposes. The highway could be freely used but not when it abused a landowner's rights.

6.4 Trespass *ab initio*

KB **Elias v Passmore** [1934] 2 KB 164

The police entered premises and seized some documents lawfully under a warrant, but also some not covered by the warrant. The claim for trespass in relation to the documents unlawfully seized was accepted but the claim of trespass *ab initio* failed.

The court held that the principle could not apply since it would have made the police liable for breaking the door to carry out the warrant.

6.5 Defences

QBD **Rigby v Chief Constable of Northamptonshire**
[1985] 2 All ER 985

Police officers fired CS gas into the claimant's shop where a dangerous armed psychopath was hiding. This ignited powder and caused the shop to burn down. The police successfully raised a defence of necessity to the claimant's action for trespass.

The court accepted that the defence was uncertain in scope but accepted that it applied in relation to the trespass because there was a life-threatening situation. (However, the police were found negligent for not providing effective fire-fighting cover.)

CHAPTER 7

TORTS CONCERNING GOODS

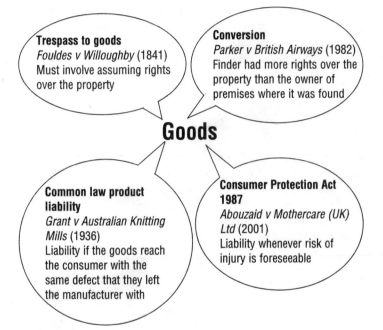

Trespass to goods
Fouldes v Willoughby (1841)
Must involve assuming rights over the property

Conversion
Parker v British Airways (1982)
Finder had more rights over the property than the owner of premises where it was found

Goods

Common law product liability
Grant v Australian Knitting Mills (1936)
Liability if the goods reach the consumer with the same defect that they left the manufacturer with

Consumer Protection Act 1987
Abouzaid v Mothercare (UK) Ltd (2001)
Liability whenever risk of injury is foreseeable

7.1 Trespass to goods

7.1.1 Trespass to goods

CE **Fouldes v Willoughby (1841) 8 M & W 540**

The claimant boarded the defendant's ferry with two horses. The claimant was alleged to have behaved improperly and so to induce him to leave the ferry the defendant took hold of the horses and led them ashore. The claimant's action failed.

The requirements of the tort were that the interference should be both direct and intentional. The court held that the defendant did not intend to interfere with the rights of the owner of the horses or assume any rights over them himself and so the action failed.

7.1.2 Conversion

CA **Parker v British Airways Board** [1982] QB 1004

The claimant found a gold bracelet in an airport lounge and handed it in together with his name and address. The true owner could not be found and the defendant air company sold it. The claimant then tried to claim the proceeds but the company refused.

The court rejected the argument that the airport should have more right to the property than the finder because the real owner was more likely to make enquiries of them. The fact that the defendant had a procedure for lost property was insufficient to establish rights over things found on its premises and it was liable for conversion and was bound to return the property to the finder.

7.2 Product liability

7.2.1 Common law liability for defective products in tort

PC **Grant v Australian Knitting Mills** [1936] All ER Rep 209

The claimant contracted a painful skin disease from chemicals in underpants that he had bought. The chemicals were a part of the manufacturing process and the processes used to remove them had failed to do so.

The court applied the basic principle in *Donoghue v Stevenson* (1932) in the claim against the manufacturer in making the defendant liable.

Lord Wright stated:
'The garments were made by the manufacturers for the purpose of being worn exactly as they were worn ... in *Donoghue* ... the essential point ...was that the article should reach the consumer or user subject to the same defect as it had when it left the manufacturer. That this was true of the garment is ... beyond question.'

7.2.2 The Consumer Protection Act 1987

CA **Abouzaid v Mothercare (UK) Ltd** [2001] EWCA Civ 348

The claimant was injured in the eye when he was fastening elastic straps to secure a sleeping bag to a pushchair. The plastic slipped through his fingers and the buckle hit him in the eye. He claimed under the Act.

The court held that the product was defective within the meaning of the Act because the design meant that the risk of injury was possible without the manufacturers giving any warning that it might occur.

CHAPTER 8

TRESPASS TO THE PERSON

Assault
Read v Coker (1853)
Requires physical actions that are threatening
Thomas v NUM (1986)
No assault if claimant could not apprehend imminent harm
Tuberville v Savage (1669)
Words used can negate the assault
R v Ireland; R v Burstow (1998)
Silent telephone calls have been accepted as assault in criminal law so words may now be sufficient for assault in tort

Battery
Letang v Cooper (1965)
Force must be applied directly and intentionally so not negligently
Wilson v Pringle (1987)
Said that hostility was also needed
Collins v Wilcock (1984)
Said it was touching that went beyond what was acceptable
In re F (Mental Patient: Sterilisation) (1990)
Medical treatment possible without consent if necessary and in patient's best interests
Lane v Holloway (1968)
Force used in self-defence must be reasonable

Trespass to the person

False imprisonment
Bird v Jones (1845)
Requires total bodily restraint with no means of escape
Meering v Graham White Aviation (1919)
Can occur even though claimant unaware of the imprisonment
Herd v Weardale Steel, Coal and Coke (1915)
No false imprisonment where there is a contractual duty to remain
Hsu v Commissioner of Police for the Metropolis (1997)
Lawful arrest is a defence but only if carried out reasonably

Wilkinson v Downton
Wilkinson v Downton (1897)
A claim is possible for harm intentionally but indirectly caused
Wainwright v Home Office (2003)
But claim not possible unless there is evidence of specific intent to cause physical or psychiatric harm

8.1 Assault

8.1.1 Definition

Read v Coker (1853) 13 CB 850

The claimant owed the defendant rent. When the defendant told the claimant to leave the premises, the claimant refused. The defendant then ordered some employees to escort the claimant from the premises. These men surrounded the claimant, rolled up their sleeves and told him that if he did not leave they would break his neck. Held that there was an assault.

The Court of Common Pleas held that there was a threat of violence with an ability to carry out the threat, indicated by the rolling up of sleeves but not by the words alone. This amounted to an actionable assault.

Byles Serjt. explained that:
'To constitute an assault, there must be something more than a threat of violence …There must be some act done denoting a present ability and an intention to assault.'

8.1.2 Ingredients of the tort

Thomas v National Union of Mineworkers [1986] 1 Ch 20

During the miners' strike in 1984–85 working miners suffered abuse from striking miners as they were taken into the colliery in buses. Their claim for an injunction to prevent the picketing failed.

The court held that there could be no assault since there was no possibility of the striking miners reaching the working miners as they were in buses at the time of the abuse. As such they could not have been put in any apprehension of an imminent battery.

CP **Tuberville v Savage** (1669) 1 Mod Rep 3

During an argument with the claimant the defendant put his hand on his sword and said: 'If it were not Assize time I would not take such language from you.' The claim of assault failed.

The court held that there was no assault because, while words alone cannot amount to an assault, they can make clear that an assault is not intended. The words here showed that the claimant had no intention to harm the claimant at that particular time so the claimant could not fear an impending battery.

HL **R v Ireland; R v Burstow** [1998] AC 147 HL

This involved joined criminal appeals on whether silence can amount to assault. In both cases the victim had suffered psychiatric harm and Ireland made numerous silent telephone calls. Burstow was in effect a 'stalker', who engaged in a long campaign of silent telephone calls and anonymous letters to a young woman with whom he had briefly gone out three years previously. The case resulted in successful convictions.

The House was first of all prepared to accept the psychiatric injuries as 'actual bodily harm' which was a necessary element of the criminal charges. It also accepted that a person who uses silence in order to produce apprehension of immediate violence in others is guilty of assault.

The case is generally taken now to mean that words alone can amount to assault. However, it is a criminal case and until such time as a tort case develops *Read v Coker* (1853) is still good law.

8.2 Battery

8.2.1 Definitions

 Letang v Cooper [1965] 1 QB 232

The claimant was sunbathing in the grounds of a hotel near to where cars were parked. The defendant negligently reversed over her legs, injuring her. The woman claimed three years later, which fell outside the limitation period for negligence, so she claimed in trespass instead but was unsuccessful.

The court held that while there was direct harm caused to the woman by the defendant's negligence, there was no intention to harm her and both were required for battery. Lord Denning felt that there was no overlap between trespass and negligence although Lord Diplock felt that there could be.

Lord Denning explained:
'The plaintiff... must also allege that he did it intentionally or negligently. If intentional, it is ... assault and battery. If negligent and causing damage, it is ... negligence.'

CA **Wilson v Pringle [1987] 2 All ER 440**

The claimant, a 13-year-old boy, suffered injuries to his hip when a school friend, as a practical joke, pulled his bag off his shoulder causing him to fall. His claim for damages failed.

The court referred to the words of Holt CJ in *Cole v Turner* (1704) Holt KB 108 where he stated that 'the least touching of another in anger is a battery', and held that hostility was a necessary element of an actionable battery. Since the harm occurred during ordinary horseplay this element was missing and the claim failed.

This view would appear to narrow the scope of battery dramatically. It would make it impossible for instance to bring battery actions against doctors who engage in treatment without the consent of the patient but who clearly would not be acting with hostility.

Collins v Wilcock [1984] 3 All ER 374: see p100

8.2.2 Ingredients of the tort

QBD **Nash v Sheen** [1953] CLY 3726

The claimant went to the defendant's hairdressing salon and asked for a 'permanent wave'. Instead she was given a 'tone rinse'. This not only dyed her hair an unpleasant colour but also caused a painful rash all over her body. The defendant was liable in battery.

The court held that the defendant had applied the tone rinse to the claimant's scalp without any consent. The essential elements of a direct intentional interference were present so there was liability.

DC **Collins v Wilcock** [1984] 3 All ER 374

A woman police officer was trying to take the name and address of a woman suspected of soliciting. When the suspect went to leave the officer took hold of her arm but did not arrest her.

The court held that, since the woman was not being arrested at the time the officer intentionally restrained her, which may otherwise have made the officer's action lawful, there was a battery.

Lord Goff said:
'since her action went beyond the generally acceptable conduct

of touching a person to engage his or her attention, it must follow … that her action constituted a battery.'

Lord Goff's definition of battery appears to be much more sensible and capable of general application than that of the Court of Appeal in *Wilson v Pringle* (1987).

8.2.3 Defences to assault and battery

CA **Condon v Basi [1985] 2 All ER 453**

The claimant suffered a broken leg in a football game after a particularly reckless and dangerous tackle by the defendant. His claim in negligence succeeded.

The court rejected the defendant's argument that the mere fact of participation in a sport automatically indicated an acceptance of the risk of harm that would relieve a defendant of any duty of care. The tackle fell out of the normal risks associated with the game and could not come within the defence of *volenti*.

It must be remembered that this is in fact a negligence case. However, the principles on consent are just as appropriate when applied to battery in a sporting context.

CA **Re T (an adult) (refusal of medical treatment) [1992] 3 WLR 782**

The claimant was injured in a car crash and needed an

emergency Caesarean section when she prematurely went into labour. As a result she needed a blood transfusion. She was a Jehovah's Witness, and refused the transfusion on religious grounds but the doctors gave it anyway. Her action in battery failed.

The court on appeal accepted that in the case the patient was delirious at the time of refusal and was acting under undue influence by her mother, so that there was an emergency situation and the doctors in giving the transfusion had acted in her best interests. The court, however, accepted the absolute right of a competent patient to refuse treatment even to the point of death.

Lord Donaldson MR stated that:
'An adult patient who ... suffers from no mental incapacity has an absolute right to choose whether to consent to medical treatment, to refuse it or to choose one rather than another of the treatments being offered.'

HL In re F (Mental Patient: Sterilisation) [1990] 2 AC 1

A 30-year-old woman in a mental institution had a mental age of about four or five but had become sexually active with another inmate. It was felt that if she became pregnant this would be disastrous for her. As contraception was inappropriate in the circumstances, the doctors applied to the court for a compulsory sterilisation. The treatment was allowed.

The House held that, despite the inability of the claimant to consent, the sterilisation would be allowed because it was in her best interests, and it based its view on the principle of necessity.

The majority of judges in both the House of Lords and the Court of Appeal felt that the treatment would have been lawful without seeking a declaration from the courts. Nevertheless the issues in medical battery are often complex and it is important that individual cases should be referred to the courts.

Re S (Adult: refusal of medical treatment) [1992] 3 WLR 806; Re C (Adult: refusal of medical treatment) [1994] 1 WLR 290.

CA **Lane v Holloway [1968] 1 QB 379**

A strained relationship existed between some neighbours. When one of them, the defendant, came home drunk and rowdy one night he was told by the woman next door to be quiet. He replied 'Shut up you monkey faced tart'. This then led to a fight between the defendant and the woman's husband. The defendant made a friendly and ineffectual shove at the husband who then beat him in the face so that he required 19 stitches. This attack was out of proportion to the gestures of the drunken man and the defence of self-defence failed.

The court held that for the defence to apply only reasonable force was appropriate. The reaction here was out of proportion to the verbal provocation by the claimant and the defence failed.

8.3 False imprisonment

8.3.1 Definition and ingredients of the tort

QB **Bird v Jones** (1845) 7 QB 742

The claimant wanted to cross Hammersmith Bridge. The footpath was closed and cordoned off for people to watch a regatta so he was invited by police officers to return the way that he had come. He refused and lost his subsequent action for false imprisonment.

The court held that for the tort to apply there must be a total bodily restraint. Since there was a way of him getting away there was no unlawful restraint and no actionable trespass.

Coleridge J suggested:
'it is one part of the definition of freedom to be able to go whither-soever one pleases; but imprisonment is something more than the mere loss of this power; it includes the notion of restraint within some limits defined by a will or power exterior to our own.'

Meering v Graham White Aviation (1919) 122 LT 44

The claimant was questioned in relation to thefts from his employer. Unknown to him, two men were posted at the door to prevent him from leaving. His claim for false imprisonment succeeded.

The court held that knowledge of the imprisonment was not an essential element of the tort and therefore as the claimant had been held without lawful cause there was indeed a false imprisonment.

Robinson v Balmain New Ferry [1910] AC 295

The claimant had entered an enclosed wharf in order to board the ferry from Sydney to Balmain. Payment of a penny was made on exiting the wharf. The claimant in fact missed the ferry and as the next ferry was not due for another 20 minutes, he wished to exit. The gate manager would not allow him to without paying a penny which he refused to do. His claim for false imprisonment failed.

The court held that there was no false imprisonment because by passing through the turnstiles the claimant had agreed to be bound by the contractual terms.

8.3.2 Defences

Herd v Weardale Steel, Coal and Coke Co. [1915] AC 67

The claimants, who were miners, had entered the mine but towards the start of their shift, decided that they were being asked to do work that was too dangerous so they asked to be returned in the cages to the surface. The employers refused and they were not allowed out until the end of their shift. Their action for false imprisonment failed.

The court held that there was no false imprisonment since the men had already contracted to stay down the mine for a specific time and the employer was not obliged to use the lift until then. This was a reasonable condition for release.

Hsu v Commissioner of Police for the Metropolis
[1997] 3 WLR 402

The claimant, who was a hairdresser, refused to allow police officers without a warrant to enter his house. He was grabbed, handcuffed, and then thrown into a police van where he was punched, kicked, and verbally abused. He was finally released from custody wearing only his jeans and flip-flops and had to walk two miles home where he found his door open and property stolen. At hospital he was found to have extensive bruising and blood in his urine. His complaint to the Police Complaints Authority succeeded and he sued successfully in trespass to the person.

The court found that there was no lawful justification for his detention and the police had not used reasonable force.

8.4 Intentional indirect harm

QBD **Wilkinson v Downton [1897] 2 QB 57**

The claimant suffered severe shock after the defendant had told her as a joke that her husband had been seriously injured in an accident. Her claim for damages succeeded.

The court held that, since there was no direct interference an action in trespass was not possible. However, the court found that there was an intentional act that was calculated to cause harm indirectly for which the defendant must be liable, since it was reasonable to assume that the harm was of a type that could be expected of a reasonable person in the circumstances.

HL **Wainwright v Home Office**
[2003] UKHL 53; [2003] 3 WLR 1137

A mother and son, the claimants, visited a prisoner in prison and were subjected to full strip searches, which were not authorised under the prison rules, in order to check for drugs. The mother suffered emotional distress as a consequence but the son suffered post traumatic stress disorder. The claimants alleged that the searches were an invasion of their privacy and also that the rule in *Wilkinson v Downton* (1897) applied. Their actions for damages failed.

The House of Lords first of all rejected the idea that there was a common law tort of invasion of privacy. Secondly, it held that the rule in *Wilkinson v Downton* (1897) could not apply without proof of a specific intention to cause either physical or psychiatric injury.

Mention was made in the case of the Prevention of Harassment Act 1997. This requires a course of action of at least two incidents so the rule in *Wilkinson v Downton* still survives for single incidents that are intentional but cause damage indirectly.

CHAPTER 9

TORTS AFFECTING REPUTATION

Defamation
Monson v Tussauds (1894)
Libel is defamation in permanent form e.g. a waxwork effigy
Theaker v Richardson (1962)
There must be a publication to a third party which could be where someone who might be expected to open mail does so
Hulton & Co v Jones (1910)
The defamation must refer to the claimant but it is sufficient that it is reasonable to suppose that acquaintances might think it refers to him
Tolley v Fry (1931)
Defamation can be by innuendo or by implication
Byrne v Deane (1937)
The statement must lower the estimation of the claimant in the minds of right thinking people so following the law would not lower that estimation
Knupffer v London Express Newspapers Ltd (1944)
Class actions usually fail unless the claimant is individually recognisable
Bookbinder v Tebbitt (1989)
The truth can never be defamatory
Kemsley v Foot (1952)
Fair comment is a defence where it is genuine opinion based on facts and in the public interest
Reynolds v Times Newspapers (2001)
Qualified privilege defence depends on ten key factors

Torts affecting reputation

Deceit
Derry v Peek (1889)
Liability possible where defendant made a false representation knowingly, without belief in its truth, or reckless as to whether it was true or not
Malicious falsehood
Kaye v Robertson (1991)
The false statement must be made maliciously and calculated to cause the claimant financial loss

9.1 Defamation

9.1.1 The categories of defamation

QBD **Monson v Tussauds Ltd** [1894] 1 QB 671

A man accused of murder was released on a 'not proven' verdict by a Scottish jury. The defendant produced a wax effigy of the man and placed it at the entrance to the Chamber of Horrors.

The court held that the effigy on its own did not amount to defamation but its juxtaposition with other tableaux in the Chamber of Horrors indicated that he was in fact guilty and thus did. Libel is defamation in permanent form and the court held that the waxwork was sufficiently permanent to be libel.

CA **Youssoupoff v MGM Pictures Ltd** (1934) 50 TLR 581

A film about the life of Rasputin suggested that he had seduced a Princess Natasha, one of the Russian Royal family, who was recognisable as the claimant.

The court held that even though the film did not suggest that the princess was at all responsible for the seduction, the suggestion was still sufficient to damage her social standing. The film was accepted as defamation in permanent form and was thus libel.

9.1.2 The essential elements of the tort

CA **Theaker v Richardson** [1962] 1 WLR 151

A member of a local council wrote a letter to another member of the council in which he called her a 'lying, low down brothel keeping whore and thief.' The claimant's husband opened and read the letter. The claimant's action for libel succeeded.

The court identified that there was a publication since it was reasonable to assume that the husband, who was the claimant's election agent, might open it, thinking it was an election address.

HL **Hulton & Co. v Jones** [1910] AC 20

A humorous fictitious article in a newspaper about the London to Dieppe motor rally suggested that the central character called Artemus Jones and described as a churchwarden from Peckham had engaged in an affair. The claimant, also called Artemus Jones, who was a barrister from Wales, sued successfully for libel.

The court held that it was not necessary to show that the defamation was intended to refer to the claimant, only that people who knew him might easily believe that the article referred to him.

HL Tolley v Fry & Sons Ltd [1931] AC 333

An advertising poster for Fry's chocolate bars included a caricature of a famous amateur golfer of the time with a bar of chocolate sticking out of his back pocket. He sued successfully in libel because he was disturbed that his amateur status would be compromised because people would think that he had been paid.

The court held that the advert was defamation by innuendo; the suggestion of breaching amateur rules was implied.

CA Byrne v Deane [1937] 1 KB 818

After a tip-off from an informer, police had removed an illegal gambling machine from a golf club. Later a poem appeared on the notice board which included the words 'he who gave the game away may he byrne in hell'. The claimant argued that the spelling was an accusation that he was the informer and suggested disloyalty on his part. His claim failed.

While there was a publication, the court held that the words were not defamatory since the inference in the poem was that the claimant had done his duty as a law-abiding citizen, which could not lower his estimation in the minds of right-thinking people.

Greene LJ was of the opinion that 'to say of a man that he has put in motion the proper machinery for suppressing crime is a thing which ... cannot, on the face of it, be defamatory'.

CA **Cassidy v Daily Mirror Newspapers Ltd** [1929] 2 KB 331

Mrs Cassidy sued successfully when a picture was taken of her husband at the races, accompanied by a young woman who was described in the caption as being recently engaged.

The court held that by innuendo the photograph implied that the young woman was Mr Cassidy's fiancé and that Mr and Mrs Cassidy were not married, which had caused and could cause her friends to doubt her moral character. It was therefore defamatory.

Russell LJ explained that:
'Liability for libel does not depend on the intention of the defamer, but on the fact of the defamation.'

Scrutton LJ added:
'If newspapers ... publish statements which may be defamatory ... without inquiry as to their truth, in order to make their newspaper more attractive, they must take the consequences if ... their statements are found to be untrue.'

HL | Knupffer v London Express Newspapers Ltd [1944] AC 116

An article about the Young Russian Party described it as
unpatriotic and being willing to help Hitler. Knupffer was
head of the British branch of the party which had only 24
members. His claim failed.

The court held that, since the party was in fact international,
no individual could be easily identified in the article and
reasonable people would not think that it referred to the
claimant in particular.

Lord Atkin explained:
'The reason why a libel published of a large or indeterminate
number of persons described by some general name generally
fails to be actionable is the difficulty of establishing that the
plaintiff was, in fact, included in the defamatory statement.'

Actions alleging defamation of a class of people will almost
always fail unless the class is so small that it is possible to
recognise the individual claimant in the class, e.g. 'Footballers
are corrupt villains' would fail, but 'The goalkeepers at
Badborough United are renowned for taking money to lose
matches' might succeed.

9.1.3 Defences

 Bookbinder v Tebbitt [1989] 1 All ER 1169

During an election campaign the defendant referred to the policies of a local council as 'a damn fool idea'. The policy in question was overprinting stationery with 'Support Nuclear Free Zone'. The defendant was unsuccessful in his defence of justification.

The court would not allow the defendant to introduce evidence of the council's overspending, so the words in context were incapable of supporting the specific allegation made by the defendant.

 Telnikoff v Matusevitch [1992] 4 All ER 817

In an article in the *Telegraph* the claimant criticised the BBC Russian Service for over-recruiting employees from ethnic minority groups. The defendant then replied in a letter to the paper accusing the claimant of being racist and anti-Semitic. The defendant successfully pleaded fair comment in the claimant's action.

The House of Lords felt that the defendant had to show that he was commenting since many people might not have seen the original article and would not necessarily know to what he was referring. On this basis the defence could only be defeated by the claimant showing malicious intent on the part of the defendant which he had not done. The claimant had also failed to disprove that the defendant had an honest belief in the view expressed.

HL Kemsley v Foot [1952] AC 345

A former leader of the Labour Party, while a junior MP, wrote an article in response to an article, attacking it as 'one of the foulest pieces of journalism perpetuated in this country for many a long year'. The article itself appeared under the headline 'Lower than Kemsley', a reference to another newspaper. The proprietor of that newspaper argued that in the light of the attack in the article the reference to his paper reflected badly on it and was defamatory.

The defence of fair comment succeeded because the article was genuine comment, supported by factual information, and was in the public interest. The headline was used as a comparison.

CA Vizetelly v Mudie's Select Library Ltd [1900] 2 QB 170

A mobile library failed to prevent circulation of a book containing defamatory material after receiving a warning about its content.

The defendants were liable because they had ignored the warnings and had failed to establish that they published innocently. The court accepted, however, that there could be a defence of innocent dissemination which would be available if defendants could show that:

- they were unaware that the book contained defamatory material when they distributed it;
- there was nothing suspicious to alert them to the presence of the defamatory material;
- there was no negligence on their part.

The defence is now probably subsumed within s 1 of the Defamation Act 1996, although not repealed by it.

HL Reynolds v Times Newspapers [2001] 2 AC 127

The claimant had been leader of the Irish parliament and was trying to promote the Northern Ireland peace process. A political crisis arose so he resigned and withdrew his party from the governing coalition. The *Sunday Times* then published an article which the claimant felt suggested that he had both misled the Irish Parliament and withheld information from it. The newspaper failed to print an apology so he claimed for libel. The newspaper sought to rely on the defence of qualified privilege but was unsuccessful.

The Court of Appeal held that qualified privilege can be argued by the press when (i) the paper has a moral, social or legal duty to inform the public of the matter in question; and (ii) the public has a corresponding interest in receiving the information; and (iii) the nature, status and source of the material and the circumstances of the publication are such as to warrant the protection of privilege. On appeal the House of Lords decided that there was no general category of qualified privilege for political information. Despite arguments based on Art 10 of the European Convention on Human Rights, the standard test of duty to disseminate and duty to receive should be applied. They held that 10 matters were critical:

- the seriousness of allegation;
- whether or not it was of public concern;
- the source of the information;
- whether steps were taken to verify it;
- the status of the information;
- the urgency of the issue;
- whether comment was sought from the claimant;
- whether the claimant's comments were included in the article;
- the tone of the article;
- the circumstances and timing of publication.

Since the article here was highly critical and the defendants had never sought the claimant's side of the story they had no privilege.

9.2 Malicious falsehood and deceit

9.2.1 Deceit

HL **Derry v Peek** (1889) 14 App Cas 337

A tram company was licensed by Act of Parliament to operate horse drawn trams. The Act also allowed use of mechanical power by gaining a certificate from the Board of Trade. The company applied for a certificate and at the same time issued a prospectus to raise further share capital. Honestly believing that the certificate would be granted, the company falsely represented in the prospectus that it was able to use mechanical power. In fact the application was denied and the company fell into liquidation. The claimant had invested on the strength of the representation in the prospectus and lost money. His action for damages failed.

The court held that there was insufficient proof of fraud, the allegation of which was simply rebutted by showing an honest belief in the statement. There was no reason for the company to suppose that their application for a certificate would be refused.

Lord Herschell defined the action as requiring actual proof that the false representation was made:
'... knowingly or without belief in its truth or recklessly careless whether it be true or false.'

9.2.2 Malicious falsehood

CA **Kaye v Robertson [1991] FSR 62**

A famous television actor, Gorden Kaye, was injured. Journalists from the *Sunday Sport* entered the actor's room, interviewed him and took photographs, even though he was in no fit state to consent. They then published the photographs and a story about his injuries, falsely stating that the story was produced with the actor's permission. His action for malicious falsehood succeeded although a claim for invasion of privacy failed.

The court accepted that the ingredients of the tort were made out. The defendant had made a false statement about the claimant to third parties by publishing the story and photographs. It was malicious in having been done while he was too ill to realise. The loss to the claimant was that it prevented him from marketing the story himself and receiving payment for it.

Wainwright v Home Office [2003] UKHL 53; [2003] 3 WLR
1137 see p107 (on invasion of privacy).

CHAPTER 10

EMPLOYMENT-RELATED TORTS

Vicarious liability
Ready Mixed Concrete v Minister of Pensions and National Insurance (1968)
The tortfeasor must be employed according to the 'economic reality' test
Poland v Parr (1927)
The employer is responsible for all authorised acts
Rose v Plenty (1976)
And prohibited acts where the employer gains a benefit
Twine v Beans Express (1946)
But not where the employee is on a 'frolic on his own'
Lister v Hesley Hall (2001)
Employer can be liable for employee's crimes where there is a close connection with the employment

Employment-related torts

Employer's liability
Wilsons & Clyde Coal Co Ltd v English (1938)
The employer owes a non-delegable duty of care to provide safe colleagues, plant and equipment, premises, and systems of work
Sutherland v Hatton and others (2002)
And now has a duty to protect the employee's psychiatric health if he is aware of the employee's susceptibility to stress
Baker v T E Hopkins (1959)
The employee can only consent to risks he is aware of and freely accepts
Jones v Livox Quarries (1952)
Employer's contributory negligence

Breach of a statutory duty
Lonrho Ltd v Shell Petroleum Co Ltd (No. 2) (1982)
Civil remedy not generally available if the statute provides a different sanction unless provison protects a class of individuals or claimant suffered damage above what the public would expect

10.1 Vicarious liability

10.1.1 Tests of employment status

HL **Mersey Docks & Harbour Board v Coggins and Griffiths (Liverpool) Ltd** [1947] AC 1

The Harbour Board hired out a crane to stevedores and a driver to operate it for them. In the contract between the Board and the stevedores the Board would still pay the driver and only they had the right to dismiss him, but during the contract he was employed by the stevedores. The crane driver negligently injured a person in the course of his work and the Harbour Board was held liable.

The court held that the Harbour Board was the crane driver's employer at the material time since it was in control of him and could not show that liability for his actions had shifted to the stevedores since, although they could tell him what to do they were not in a position to tell him how to operate the crane.

Lord Porter explained the control test:
'To ascertain who is the employer at any particular time ... ask who is entitled to tell the employee the way in which he is to do the work upon which he is engaged... it is not enough that the task to be performed should be under his control, he must control the method of performing it'.

QBD **Ready Mixed Concrete (South East) Ltd v Minister of Pensions and National Insurance**
[1968] 2 QB 497

Under a new contract drivers were bound to have vehicles in the company colours and logo that they also bought on hire purchase agreements from the company. They also had to maintain the vehicles according to set standards and could only use the lorries on company business. Hours were flexible, however, and pay was subject to an annual minimum rate according to the concrete hauled. The contract also permitted them to hire drivers in their place. The case concerned who was liable for National Insurance contributions: the company or one of its drivers.

The court held that the terms of the contract were inconsistent with a contract of employment and the driver was self-employed.

McKenna J developed the 'economic reality' test: '(i) The servant agrees that in consideration of a wage or other remuneration he will provide his own work and skill in the performance of some services ... (ii) he agrees, expressly or impliedly, that in the performance of that service he will be in the other's control in a sufficient degree to make that other master; (iii) the other provisions of the contract are consistent with it being a contract of service.'

10.1.2 Tort occurring in the course of employment

 Poland v Parr [1927] 1 KB 236

The employee was a carter who assaulted a boy in order to stop him from stealing from his employer's wagon. The boy fell under the wagon and was injured as a result.

The court held that, while the act was excessive and thus tortious, since the employee was only protecting the employer's property, and by implication he had authority to do so, the employer would be vicariously liable for the employee's act.

Atkin LJ explained:
'Any servant is, as a general rule, authorised to do acts which are for the protection of his master's property.'

CA **Rose v Plenty** [1976] 1 WLR 141

A milkman used a child helper despite the express instructions of his employer not to allow people to ride on the milk floats. The boy was then injured through the milkman's negligent driving.

The court held that the milkman was carrying out his work in an unauthorised manner but was still in the course of his employment because the employer benefited from the work done by the boy.

Lord Denning explained that:
'An employer's express prohibition … is not necessarily such
as to exempt the employer from liability, provided that the act
is done not for the employee's own purpose, but in the course
of his service and for his employer's benefit.'

HL **Century Insurance Co. Ltd v Northern Ireland
Transport Board [1942] AC 509**

A driver of a petrol tanker was delivering to a petrol station.
He lit a cigarette and carelessly threw down the lit match,
causing an explosion and extensive damage. The employer was
held liable.

The court held that the driver was in the course of
employment because he was engaged in his primary activity,
delivering petrol, and was merely doing his work in a
negligent manner.

CA **Twine v Beans Express [1946] 1 All ER 202**

A hitchhiker was injured through the negligence of a driver
who was expressly forbidden to give lifts. The employers were
not liable.

The court held that the driver was doing something outside of
his contract in giving free lifts and that the express prohibition
was also a limiting factor on the scope of his employment.

CA **Viasystems (Tyneside) Ltd v Thermal Transfer (Northern) Ltd [2005] EWCA Civ 1151**

A fitter's mate who was seconded by his employers to other contractors negligently flooded a factory floor.

The court held that, because both employers were both entitled and obliged to control the worker to prevent negligent acts, both could be vicariously liable for his actions.

10.1.3 Liability for the crimes of employees

HL **Lister v Hesley Hall Ltd [2001] 2 All ER 769**

The claimants were residents in a school for children with emotional difficulties. They were all sexually abused over time by the warden who was later convicted of criminal charges. The claimants sought damages against the school on the basis that it had actual or constructive knowledge of the abuse and failed to prevent it.

The House of Lords rejected the test in *Trotman v North Yorkshire County Council* (1999) LGR 584 and held that the appropriate test was whether there was sufficient connection between the employment and the torts carried out by the employee. Here the torts were carried out on the school's premises and at times when the employee should have been caring for the claimants. The court accepted that there was an inherent risk of abuse that the employer should have guarded against so that vicarious liability was appropriate in the circumstances.

Rosalind Coe (in '*Lister v Hesley Hall Ltd*' (2002) 65 MLE 270) suggests '*Lister* has inevitably raised concerns as to the application of the "close connection" test, provoking comment that … Litigants, their advisers and insurers will all be concerned as to the boundaries of the decision and will turn to the judgments of the House for guidance. Unfortunately they will find limited assistance.'

HL **Lloyd v Grace Smith & Co.** [1912] AC 716

Solicitors employed an unsupervised conveyancing clerk. The clerk fraudulently induced a client to convey her property over to him.

The court identified that the clerk was engaged in the job that he was hired to do and that the fraud occurred because he was given insufficient supervision by his employers who were thus liable.

10.1.4 The employer's indemnity

HL **Lister v Romford Ice & Cold Storage Ltd** [1957] AC 555

A lorry driver negligently knocked over his father who was acting as his driver's mate. The father claimed compensation from the employers whose insurers on settling the claim exercised their rights of subrogation under the insurance contract by suing the driver.

The House of Lords accepted that this was possible.

The case was very strongly criticised, not least because it destroys the purpose of imposing vicarious liability. Because of this insurers are reluctant to exercise their rights in such an unfair way.

10.1.5 Vicarious liability of lenders of cars

HL **Morgans v Launchbury [1973] AC 127**

A wife let her husband use her car, knowing that he was going out drinking after he promised her that he would not drive while drunk. The husband drank too much, so he let a friend drive him home who was also drunk and uninsured, and who caused an accident. The Court of Appeal imposed vicarious liability on the wife so that a claim could be made against her insurance.

Lord Denning held that the fact the wife had given permission to her husband to use the car was enough to make her responsible. The House of Lords rejected this argument because it was impossible to pinpoint the exact basis on which to fix liability in the circumstances and it was not for judges to interfere with the interrelationship between liability and insurance.

10.2 Employers' liability

10.2.1 The employers' non-delegable duty

Wilsons & Clyde Coal Co Ltd v English [1938] AC 57

Colliery owners tried to delegate their responsibilities and liability under various industrial safety laws to their manager by contractually making him entirely responsible for safety. When a miner was injured the owners tried to avoid liability on this basis.

The court held the colliers liable on the basis that their personal liability could not be delegated to a third party, who was in any case an employee. The duty of care included: the duty to provide competent working colleagues; safe plant and equipment; a safe place of work; and a safe system of work.

CA **Bux v Slough Metals** [1974] 1 All ER 262

In compliance with health and safety regulations an employee was provided with safety goggles but would not use them because he claimed that they misted up. The employer knew this. The employee was then injured by a splash of molten metal.

The court held the employer liable for failing to ensure that the goggles were worn, identifying that the duty is not just to provide safe working systems but to ensure that they are followed.

Pape v Cumbria CC [1992] 3 All ER 211 where there was breach of a duty to warn that not wearing gloves could lead to dermatitis.

10.2.2 Developments in the common law duty

QBD **Walker v Northumberland CC** [1995] 1 All ER 737

A senior social worker had already suffered a nervous breakdown as a result of work related stress. On returning to work he had been promised that his workload would reduce but was actually faced with a huge backlog of work from his absence. The result was that he suffered a second breakdown causing him to leave work permanently after he was dismissed on sickness grounds. His claim was successful. Leave for an appeal to the Court of Appeal was granted but the case was settled beforehand for £175,000.

The court held that the employer was liable because after the first breakdown it was aware of his susceptibility to stress and failed to reduce his workload or the pressure associated with it, and thus placed him under even more stressful conditions.

Colman J explained the development:
'It is clear law that an employer has a duty to provide his employee with a safe system of work and to take reasonable steps to protect him from risks which are reasonably foreseeable … there is no logical reason why risk of psychiatric damage should be excluded from the … duty.'

CA | **Sutherland v Hatton and others [2002] EWCA Civ 76**

This case was in fact a number of joined appeals on stress-related illnesses at work. Two claimants were teachers; one was a local authority administrator and one was a factory worker. All were claiming that they were forced to stop work because of stress-related psychiatric illnesses caused by their employers.

The appeals were decided on whether the injuries were foreseeable but the court also issued important guidelines on stress claims:

- the basic principles of negligence must apply including the usual principles of employers' liability;
- the critical question for the court to answer is whether the type of harm suffered was foreseeable;
- foreseeability depends on what the reasonable employer knew or ought reasonably to have known;
- an employer can assume that an employee can cope with the normally pressures of the work unless the employer has specific knowledge that an employee has a particular problem;
- the same test should apply whatever the employment;
- the employer should take steps to prevent possible harm when possibility of harm would be obvious to a reasonable employer;
- the employer will be liable if he then fails to take steps that are reasonable in the circumstances to avoid the harm;
- the nature of the employment, the employer's available resources, the counselling and treatment services provided are all relevant in determining whether the employer has taken effective steps to avoid the harm, and in any case the employer is only expected to take steps that will do some good;

- the employee must show that the employer's breach of duty caused the harm not merely that the harm is stress related;
- where there is more than one cause of the harm the employer will only be liable for that portion of damages that relates to the harm actually caused by his breach of duty;
- damages should take account of any pre-existing disorder.

Andrew Collender QC in 'Stress in the work place' *New Law Journal* 22 February, 2003 pp 248 and 250 discusses a problem recognised by the court:

'whilst it is possible to identify some jobs that are intrinsically physically dangerous, it is rather more difficult to identify which jobs are intrinsically so stressful that physical or psychological harm is to be expected more often than in other jobs.'

Barber v Somerset CC [2004] UKHL 13: a further appeal to HL from one of the appeals in *Hatton*.

10.2.3 Defences

CA **Baker v T E Hopkins [1959] 3 All ER 225**

Workmen were put in danger by being exposed to petrol fumes in a confined space when the fumes overcame the men. A doctor attempted to rescue the men but died himself through exposure to the fumes. The employer tried to claim *volenti* but failed.

The court held that the defence could not apply. The doctor had not agreed to the specific risks involved. He was trying to do his best for the unconscious men and did not consent to the risk of death.

The Court of Appeal explained the application of the defence by referring to the judgment of Cardozo J in an American case *Wagner v International Railway Co*:

'Danger invites rescue. The law does not ignore these reactions … in tracing conduct to its consequences. It recognises them as normal. It places their effects within the range of the natural and the probable. The wrong that imperils life … is a wrong also to the rescuer.'

CA **Jones v Livox Quarries Ltd** [1952] 2 QB 608

An employee was injured in a collision caused by the defendant's negligent driving while he was riding on the towbar of a traxcavator despite the express prohibition of his employer.

The court held that the employee had contributed to his own injury by ignoring safety instructions and reduced his damages by 5 per cent.

Lord Denning said:
'contributory negligence does not depend on a duty of care [it] does depend on foreseeability … as … negligence requires …

foreseeability of harm to others … contributory negligence requires … foreseeability of harm to oneself.'

10.3 Breach of a statutory duty

HL **Lonrho Ltd v Shell Petroleum Co Ltd (No. 2)** [1982] AC 173

The claimant argued that it suffered damage following a breach by the defendant of an Order in Council on trading with an illegal regime, in Southern Rhodesia. The order provided criminal sanctions.

The court held that there was no civil liability intended in the order so the claim failed. Lord Diplock also established the modern test for determining whether there is civil liability: It should be presumed that if the Act creates an obligation enforceable in a specific manner then it is not enforceable in any other manner, i.e. the presence of criminal sanctions usually indicate that there is no civil liability. Two exceptions are: where an obligation or prohibition is imposed by the Act to benefit a particular class of individuals; and where a provision in the Act creates a public right but the claimant suffered substantial damage different from that common to the rest of the public.

It has been argued that this gives the court too much discretion in determining how to define a particular class, and there does not appear to be a particular principle to determine the distinction between a statute creating a public right and one merely prohibiting what was previously lawful.

CA Cullen v Chief Constable of the Royal Ulster Constabulary [2003] 1 WLR 1763

Cullen was arrested then, under s 15 Northern Ireland (Emergency Provisions) Act 1987, was denied the right to see a solicitor. He was later given access to a solicitor and pleaded guilty to criminal charges. He sought damages for the delay in access to a solicitor.

The trial judge and the Northern Ireland Court of Appeal held that the police had reasonable grounds to delay access and although they had breached the statutory requirement to give the claimant reasons for this delay at the time this did not give rise to an action in tort. The House of Lords upheld the decision and also identified that there was no civil law duty because judicial review was available. The House also commented that there was no issue under the Human Rights Act 1998 as there was no breach of Art 5 or Art 6 of the European Convention on Human Rights.

CHAPTER 11

THE GENERAL DEFENCES

11.1 *Volenti non fit injuria*

HL **Smith v Baker** [1891] AC 325

A quarry worker was injured when a crane moved rocks over his head and some fell on him. He had previously complained that the practice was dangerous and the defendant argued that the fact that he continued to work meant that he had voluntarily accepted the risk of harm. The defence failed.

The House held that, while the workman may have consented to general dangers relating to his work he could not be said to have accepted the risk of the specific harm suffered.

Lord Halsbury LC explained:
'a person who relies on the maxim must shew a consent to the particular thing done … It appears to me that the proposition upon which the defendants must rely must be a far wider one than is involved in the maxim.'

11.2 Inevitable accident

QBD **Stanley v Powell [1891] 1 QB 86**

During a pheasant shoot the defendant 'accidentally' shot a beater, a man whose role it was to beat the ground so that the birds would fly up out of the moorland. The defendant successfully claimed an inevitable accident because he was able to show that the injury was caused when the pellet ricocheted off trees.

The court held that if the claimant was unable to show that the defendant acted negligently then the damage must have occurred accidentally which therefore provided a complete defence.

11.3 Act of God

CA **Nichols v Marsland (1876) 2 ExD 1**

The defendant had created artificial lakes on his land. During an exceptionally heavy rain storm described as 'the worst in living memory' the lakes burst their banks and flooded neighbouring land.

The court held that the defendant should not be liable if the escape occurred through reasons beyond his own fault but by Act of God.

11.4 Illegality (*ex turpi causa non oritur actio*)

CA **Revill v Newbery** [1996] QB 567

An allotment holder, the defendant, fed up with trespassers on his allotment, lay in wait in his shed and then fired through a hole in the door at a trespasser, injuring him. The defendant's claim, that the illegal actions of the trespasser relieved him of all liability, failed.

The court held that the defendant's actions were out of proportion in the circumstances and the defence would fail. One reason was that this would thwart the clear intentions of Parliament in the Occupiers' Liability Act 1984 to create a duty of care towards trespassers.

Evans LJ suggested that if the defence were to apply in such circumstances:
'it would mean that the trespasser … was effectively an outlaw, who was debarred by the law from recovering compensation for any injury which he might sustain.'

The extent to which a person is entitled to protect his property from trespassers is very contentious with the public. The Government is currently looking at the possibility of giving greater rights to the owners of land against trespassers.

11.5 Contributory negligence

CA **Froom v Butcher** [1976] QB 286

A car accident was caused by the defendant's negligence but the claimant was not wearing a seat belt. He suffered head and chest injuries. His claim succeeded but damages were reduced by 20 per cent.

The court applied an objective standard of care in determining that the claimant had worsened the injuries. A prudent person would have worn a seat belt, so damages were reduced by 20 per cent.

The judgment was at a time when reduction in damages was being used to persuade people to wear seat belts. The introduction of criminal charges has undoubtedly been more of a deterrent to failing to wear seat belts. Lord Denning's apportionment of blame also seems quite arbitrary.

INDEX

accident, inevitable 137
act of a stranger 44, 58, 67
  defence, strict liability 70, 79
act of God 137
allurements 47, 48–9, 55
animals, liability for 70, 80–4
Animals Act 1971 70, 80–4
'Anns' test 5–6, 40
assault 95
  defences against 101–5
  definition 96, 98
  intention to cause harm 97, 99
  silence 97–8

balance
  enjoyment of property 62
  of risk 12
  rights of public 65, 66
battery 95
  defences against 101–5
  definitions 98–9, 100–1
  direct intentional interference 100
  hostility 99
  medical cases 102–3
breach of a statutory duty 121,
  134–5
breach of duty of care 3, 5
  employers 17–18, 19–20
  novus actus interveniens 23–5
  omissions 44–6
  professionals 14–17, 18
  'reasonable man' test 3, 8–9, 11
  remoteness of damage 26–30
  standard of care 9–14
  third parties 44–5
'but for' test 3, 17–18, 23

causation 3
  break in chain 3, 23–5

'but for' test 17–18, 23
  in fact 17–23
  loss of chance of recovery 22
  loss of earnings 20–1
  no single party responsible 19–20
chain of causation 3, 23–5
children
  human rights 1–2
  occupiers' liability 47, 48–50,
    54–6
Children Act 1989 2
civil liability 134–5
classes of person 69, 114, 134
'close connection' test 126–7
common duty of humanity 47, 54
common law liability
  defective goods 93
  psychiatric illness 130–2
  trespassers 54–5
consent 47, 100, 101
  to medical treatment 102–3
  to risk 78, 81
Consumer Protection Act 1987 91,
  93–4
continuity of nuisance 63, 71
contract law 4
contributory negligence 55, 133–4,
  139
'control' test, employment status
  122
conversion, goods 92

damage to property
  necessity 90
  nuisance 59–60
dangerous animals 70, 80–2
deceit 109, 118–19
defamation 109, 111–14
  categories of 110

classes of person 114
defences against 115–18
Defamation Act 1996 117
defences against tort
  act of God 137
  assault and battery 101–4
  contributory negligence 139
  defamation 115–18
  illegality 138
  inevitable accident 137
  nuisance 65–8
  private nuisance 65–8
  strict liability 78–80
    animals 84
  trespass to land 90
  volenti non fit injuria 136
'direct and natural consequences' test
  26, 30
disabled people
  standard of care 11
duty of care 3, 4–7 *see also* breach of
  duty of care
  employers 19–20, 121, 129–30
  manufacturers 4–5
  proximity between parties 5–6
  tests for 6–7
  to trespassers 138

economic loss 3, 39–40
'economic reality' test 121, 123
emergency situation
  standard of care 12
employee crimes 126–7
employers
  duty of care 19–20, 121, 129–30
  indemnity 127–8
  liability 121
    defences against 132–4
    employee crimes 126–7
    non-delegable duty 129–30
    psychiatric injury 130–2
employment
  breach of statutory duty 134–5
  employer's liability 129–34
  status, tests of 121, 122–3
  vicarious liability 122–8
enjoyment of property 58, 59–60,
  62, 66

escape from
  owner's control 76
    animals 80, 81–4
  owner's land 71–2, 74–5
European Convention on Human
  Rights 117–18, 135
ex turpi causa non oritur actio 138
exclusion clauses 53–4

failure to act 3
'fair, just and reasonable' test 6
fair comment 115–16
false imprisonment 95, 104–5
  defence against 106–7
'floodgates' argument 30, 34
foreseeability of harm 3, 9, 10, 26,
  50, 80
  breach of duty of care 5
  duty of care 6
  neighbour principle 4
  remoteness of damage 26–30, 77
  stress-related illness 130–2
  strict liability 70
  'thin skull' rule 30

goods 91
  Consumer Protection Act 1987
    91, 93–4
  defective products 93
  rights of finder 92
  trespass to 91–2
Guard Dogs Act 1995 82

harm *see* foreseeability of harm;
  intention to cause harm
health and safety 5, 17–18, 19–20,
  129–30
highway, used for trespass 88–9
human rights 1–2, 117–18, 135

illegality, as defence 138
'immediate aftermath' test 33, 36
immunity from liability
  public bodies 2
independent contractors
  occupiers' liability 47, 51–3
inevitable accident 137
innocent dissemination 116–17

insurance 13
intention to cause harm 95, 97,
   98–9
   indirect 107–8
invasion of privacy 107–8, 119–20

'Kennedy' test 31, 32
knowledge of nuisance 63–4, 67

land
   definition 85, 87–9
   non-natural use 70, 71–4, 75, 78
   right to enjoyment 59–60
lawful visitors 47, 48–54
learner driver
   standard of care 13
lender, vicarious liability 128
liability
   human rights 1–2
   principles 1
   public bodies 2
   specialist advice 15, 40–4
libel 110–11
local authorities
   duty of care to tenant 5–6
   knowledge of nuisance 63–4
   liability for economic loss 39–40
   negligence 2
      as occupier 49–50, 53, 55–6

malice 1, 58, 61
malicious falsehood 109, 119
manufacturers
   duty of care 4–5
   product liability 93–4
medical standard of care 9–10,
      14–17, 22
   'but for' test 17–18, 23
   defence against battery 102–3
   unforeseen consequences 42–3
motive, irrelevant 1

'narrow ratio' 4
necessity, defence against trespass 90
negligence 3, 8
   assault and battery 98–9
   causation 17–25
      break in chain 25
      contributory 55, 133–4, 139

duty of care 3, 4–6
   economic loss 39–40
   foreseeable consequence 5
   limitation period 98
   negligent misstatement 40–4
   nervous shock 30–8
   omissions 44–6
   public bodies 2, 7
   'reasonable man' test 8–9
   remoteness of damage 26–30
      as separate tort 4–5
   standard of care 5, 9–14
      skilled persons 14–17
negligent misstatement 40–4
'neighbour principle' 4
nervous shock 3, 30
   'immediate aftermath' test 33, 36
   'Kennedy' test 31, 32
   primary victims 3, 31–2, 35
   secondary victims 3, 33–4, 35,
      38, 39
   single traumatic event 36–8
non-natural use of land 70, 71–4,
   75, 78
novus actus interveniens 3, 23–5
nuisance
   authorised by Parliament 68
   continuity 63, 71
   defences against 65–8
   knowledge of 63–4, 67
   private 58, 59–68, 76
   public 58, 69

occupier, definition of 47, 48
occupiers' liability 47
   defences against 53–4, 56–7
   lawful visitors
      children 48–50
      trades persons and contractors
         50–3
   trespassers 54–5
Occupiers' Liability Act 1957 47,
   49, 51, 53
Occupiers' Liability Act 1984 47,
   54–6, 138
omissions 3, 44–6

parental responsibility 47, 49
personal injury

private nuisance 76, 78
strict liability 70, 76, 79
planning permission
defence in nuisance 68
police
'three-part' test 7
trespass 89–90, 106–7
prescription period 66
Prevention of Harassment Act 1997
108
primary victims 3, 31–2, 35
privacy, invasion of 107–8, 119–20
private nuisance 58, 59–65, 76
defences against 65–8
remedies 68
right to land 59
'privity fallacy' 4
product liability 93–4
professional
advice, skilled person 40–4
opinion 3, 16–17
standard of care 14–16
proximity between parties 5
'duty of care' test 5–6, 7
psychiatric injury 30
actual bodily harm 98
clinical depression 38
employer's duty of care 121,
130–2
'Kennedy' test 31
recognised condition 3, 37
public bodies
immunity from liability 2
negligence 2, 7
public nuisance 69
public rights 2, 65, 66, 134
pure economic loss 3, 39–40

qualified privilege 117–18

'reasonable man' test 3, 8–9, 11, 78
skilled persons 41
religious conviction 102
remoteness of damage
direct and natural consequences
test 26, 30
foreseeability 27–9
strict liability 76–8
'thin skull' rule 30, 35

reputation 109
deceit 118–19
defamation 110–18
malicious falsehood 119
responsibility for advice 15, 40–4
rights
enjoyment of land 59–60
of occupation 86
over goods 91–2
public 2, 65, 66, 134
risk see also foreseeability of harm
balance of 12
consent to 76, 81, 83–4

secondary victims 3, 33–4, 35, 39
self-defence 103–4
shock see nervous shock
silence, as assault 97–8
skilled persons 14–17, 40–4
specific intent to cause harm 95
sport
nuisance 64, 66
'reasonable man' test 11
risks of harm 101
standard of care 10–11, 13–14
standard of care 9–14 see also
'reasonable man' test
disabled people 11
emergencies 12
medical cases 9–10, 14–16
owed by professionals 14–17
sport 10–11, 13–14
unqualified persons 13
statutory authority
defence in nuisance 67
defence in strict liability 70
statutory duty 79
breach of 121, 134–5
strict liability 70, 71–5
defences against 70, 78–80
exceptions for animals 81–3
foreseeability of risk 76–8
or negligence 75, 77

'thin skull' rule 30, 35
third party damage 45–6
'three-part' test
duty of care 6–7
secondary victims 33–4

trades persons
  occupiers' liability 47, 50–1
trespass *ab initio* 89
trespass to goods 91–2
trespass to land 85, 86–7
  ab initio 89
  defence against 90
  definition of land 87–9
trespass to the person 95
  assault 96–8
  battery 98–101
  defences against 101–4, 106–7
  false imprisonment 104–5
  intentional direct harm 107–8
trespassers
  occupiers' liability to 47, 54–7
  police 90

unqualified person
  standard of care 13

vicarious liability 121
  crimes of employees 126–7
  during employment 124–6
  employer's indemnity 127–8
  employment status 122–3
  lenders of cars 128
volenti 7, 47, 101, 132
volenti non fit injuria 53–4, 57, 136

warning signs 47, 53–4, 55–7